Tales of Mysti

Oneworld's Mysticism Series includes:

Edwin A. Abbott. *Flatland: A Parable of Spiritual Dimensions*

Brother Lawrence. *The Practice of the Presence of God*

R. A. Nicholson. *Rūmī, Poet & Mystic*

Geoffrey Parrinder. *Mysticism in the World's Religions*

Margaret Smith. *Studies in Early Mysticism in the Near and Middle East*

Margaret Smith. *Rābi'a: The Life and Work of Rābi'a and Other Women Mystics in Islam*

Evelyn Underhill. *Mysticism: The Nature and Development of Spiritual Consciousness*

Evelyn Underhill. *The Spiritual Life: Great Spiritual Truths for Everyday Life*

Evelyn Underhill. *Concerning the Inner Life*

Evelyn Underhill. *The Essentials of Mysticism*

W. M. Watt. *The Faith and Practice of Al-Ghazāli*

R. C. Zaehner. *Hindu & Muslim Mysticism*

Tales of Mystic Meaning

Selections from the Mathnawī of Jalāl-ud-Dīn Rūmī

Translated with an Introduction by
REYNOLD A. NICHOLSON

ONEWORLD
OXFORD

Tales of Mystic Meaning

Oneworld Publications
(Sales and Editorial)
185 Banbury Road
Oxford OX2 7AR
England

Oneworld Publications
(U.S. Marketing Office)
42 Broadway
Rockport, MA 01966
U.S.A.

ISBN 1–85168–097–7

Printed and bound in Finland by WSOY

Did I Not Tell You . . .

Did I not tell you, "Do not leave, for I am your Friend!"?
For in this mirage of nothingness I am the Fountainhead of Life!

Even if in anger you leave Me for a hundred thousand years,
In the end you will return, for I am your true Goal!

Did I not tell you, "Be not content with worldly forms!"?
For I am the Fashioner of the tabernacle of your contentment!

Did I not tell you, "I am the Sea and you are but a single fish"?
Do not be tempted ashore, for I am your Crystal Sea!

Did I not tell you, "Do not fly like a bird to the snare!"?
Come to Me, for I am the very Power of your flight!

Did I not tell you, "They will rob you and leave you numb with cold"?
But I am the Fire and Warmth and Heat of your desire!

Did I not tell you, "They will taint your character,
Until you forget that I am your Source of Purity"?

Did I not tell you, "Do not question how I direct your affairs!"?
For I am the Creator without directions.

If your heart is a lamp, let it lead you to your true path.
And if you are godly, know that I am your Lord!

Rūmī

CONTENTS

CONTENTS

INTRODUCTION

I

THE conquest of Persia by the Arabs produced,
among other things, an Islamic literature in
the Persian language, very different in character
from the contemporary Arabic literature (though
of course they have much in common), and
expressing unmistakably the genius of the gifted
race which *capta ferum victorem cepit*. Of this
literature the best part, in every meaning of the
phrase, was composed by poets; and for a
thousand years Persian poetry has been the chief
interpreter of Persian thought to other peoples,
both in the East and the West. Its first triumphs
were won in the fields of epic and romance. If
Firdawsī may not be compared with Homer,
the *Shāhnāma* nevertheless is a worthy monu-
ment to the Heroic Age of Iran, from Jamshīd,
who "gloried and drank deep," and Rustam, the
unwitting slayer of his own son, through Darius
and Alexander the Great down to the rise of the
Sāsānian Empire with Ardashīr Bābakān and

its fall in the reign of Yazdigird. While this great
national poem finds admirers in many nations,
the romantic masterpieces of Nizāmī are dis-
appointing when translated; the style is too
subtle and obscure, the treatment of the subject
too conventional, to appeal strongly to us.
Meanwhile the art of panegyric had culminated
in Anwarī, and the quatrain or *rubāʿī* had established itself as the vehicle for epigrammatic—in
the Greek sense—criticism of life. The collec-
tion attributed to Omar Khayyām resembles the
Greek Anthology in being the work of various
more or less eminent hands, known and un-
known, early and late. The extent of Omar's
share in it is uncertain. Very few of the *rubāʿiyāt*
can be definitely assigned to him, and a great
number of them cannot possibly be his; but,
taken together, they present characteristic ideas
with such simplicity and elegance that we may
excuse Fitzgerald for having made their reputed
author by far the most famous and popular of all
Persian writers in the Western literary world.
Besides epic, romance, panegyric, and epigram,
there was another type of poetry—the mystical
and ethical—which had been gaining ground
from the eleventh century onwards, and, after

the Mongol Invasion, not only eclipsed its rivals but attained an almost absolute supremacy in its own kind. Drawing inspiration from the religious philosophy of the Sūfīs, it seeks to shadow forth, in beautiful symbolic imagery, the emanation of all things from God and their ultimate re-union with Him, the longing of the mystic lover for the Beloved, his inward purification and transformation through suffering, his ecstasies and despairs—and, when the last veil has fallen away, his seeing "with the eye of certainty" that there is no "other" and that the Truth is essentially One. We need not discuss here the spiritual love-lyrics and wine-songs which were often chanted, with or without an accompaniment of music, in order to rouse emotion and induce ecstasy, and in some cases were composed with that object. Many Sūfīs were teachers as well as enthusiasts. In their didactic works the transcendental aspects of the doctrine may occupy an unimportant place or, at least, be combined with "a loftily inculcated ethical system, which recognises in charity, purity of heart, self-renunciation, and bridling of the passions the necessary conditions of eternal happiness." Among *mathnawīs* (poems

xiii

in rhymed couplets) of this class the *Hadīqatu
'l-Haqīqat*, or "Garden of Truth," by Sanā'ī
of Ghazna and the *Mantiqu 't-Tayr* or "Bird-
Speech" by 'Attār of Nīshāpūr deserve mention
on their merits, and also because Jalālu'ddīn
Rūmī, the author of "The Mathnawī" *par
excellence*, regarded Sanā'ī and 'Attār as his
masters in Sūfism.

II

Born at Balkh in 1207, Jalālu'ddīn belonged
to a family claiming descent from the Caliph
Abū Bakr and allied with the royal house of
Khwārazm (Khiva), his grandfather having
married a daughter of Sultān Muhammad
Khwārazmshāh. In 1206 this monarch annexed
Balkh to his empire. At that time he was a
zealous Sunnī, and he is so described in one of
the stories in the *Mathnawī* (see p. 128 *infra*);
but soon afterwards he embraced the Shī'ite
heresy, a step that must have been bitterly re-
sented by the orthodox citizens of Balkh, in-
cluding the poet's father, Bahā'u'ddīn Walad,
a man distinguished for piety and learning. We
are told that Bahā'u'ddīn incurred the wrath
of Khwārazmshāh and left the city, accompanied
by his family, when Jalālu'ddīn was still a child.
After long wanderings, in the course of which
they visited Baghdād, Mecca, and Damascus,
the exiles arrived in Rūm (Asia Minor), and
finally settled at Qōniya (Iconium) under the
protection of the Seljūq Sultān 'Alā'u'ddīn
Kayqubād. Here Jalālu'ddīn spent the last fifty

years of his life, whence he is known as "Rūmī."
He died in 1273, leaving two sons and a
daughter.

If one can scarcely think of Plato without
Socrates, still less is it possible to separate
Jalālu'ddīn Rūmī from Shams-i Tabrīz, the
mysterious dervish under whose name he published his *Dīwān* and with whom he identified
himself so intimately that the very existence of
his *alter ego* has been doubted, in my opinion
unwarrantably. The history of Sūfism affords
many examples of enthusiastic friendship between teachers and disciples, and the *Mathnawī*
shows that after the death of Shams-i Tabrīz
the poet stood in a similar mystic relation to
Husāmu'ddīn Chelebi, who succeeded him as
Head of the Mevlevī Order of Dervishes—the
Order founded by Jalālu'ddīn in memory, it is
said, of Shams-i Tabrīz, with "their tall drab-
coloured felt hats and wide cloaks," their reed-
flutes and rebecks, and their whirling dance.
It was a wild flock that he and the inner group
of saintly men who gathered round him at
Qōniya were called upon to shepherd. Such a
task demanded immense energy, experience,
and knowledge of the world. That he composed

most of his poetry while engaged in organising and directing the affairs of a great Brotherhood would be incredible if we did not know, from St. Paul, for instance, what strength is given by the union of deep mystical faith with an intense and creative personality.

III

The *Mathnawī*, frequently described as the *Qur'ān-i Pahlawī* or *Qur'ān* of Persia, belongs to the last period of his life, and was begun at the request of his favourite disciple, Husā-mu'ddīn Chelebi, who acted as amanuensis. Its six Books were composed at intervals during approximately fifteen years, and in the oldest manuscripts amount to rather less than 26,000 verses; in the Persian and Indian editions this total is greatly increased by interpolations. The author died before finishing the Sixth Book. The so-called Seventh Book was added in the seventeenth century by Ismā'īl Anqiravī, who wrote a Turkish commentary on the poem. Books I and II have been translated by Sir James Redhouse[1] and Dr. C. E. Wilson[2] respectively, and a complete version by the present writer is in course of publication.[3] The contents

---

[1] *The Mesnevī of Mevlānā Jelālu'd-dīn Muhammed er-Rūmī. Book the First. . . . Translated and the poetry versified by James W. Redhouse. (London, 1881.)*

[2] *The Masnavī by Jalālu'd-dīn Rūmī. Book II translated for the first time from the Persian into prose, with a Commentary, by C. E. Wilson. (London, 1910.)*

[3] *The Mathnawī of Jalālu'ddīn Rūmī. Edited from the*

of the work are excellently summarised by E. H. Whinfield.[1] With all its faults—and from a modern point of view they are many—the *Mathnawī* exhibits, more fully than the *Dīwān-i Shams-i Tabrīz*, the marvellous range of Jalālu'ddīn's poetical genius. His *Odes* reach the utmost heights of which a poetry inspired by vision and rapture is capable, and these alone would have made him the unchallenged laureate of Mysticism. But they move in a world remote from ordinary experience, open to none but "the unveiled," whereas the *Mathnawī* is chiefly concerned with problems and speculations bearing on the conduct, use, and meaning of Life. While the *Odes* depict Reality as reflected in the clairvoyant consciousness of the Saint, the *Mathnawī* represents the Saint not only as a mirror of Reality, but also as a personage invested with Divine authority and power, an indispensable Guide on the Way to God, a Physician who can diagnose and cure diseases of the

oldest *manuscripts available, with critical notes, translation and commentary, by R. A. Nicholson. E. J. W. Gibb Memorial Fund, New Series, IV. (London and Leiden, 1925—.)*

[1] *Masnavī-i Ma'navī, the Spiritual Couplets of Manlānā Jalālu'd-dīn Muhammed Rūmī, translated and abridged by E. H. Whinfield. (London, 1887; 2nd ed., 1898.)*

soul, a Preacher of the Truth and a Teacher
of the Law—the law of reverent obedience,
through which "Heaven was filled with light
and the Angels became pure and holy." Pro-
fessing to expound the esoteric doctrine of the
Qur'ān, this vast rambling discourse provides
instruction and entertainment for all seekers.
Few would care to read it through; but everyone can find in it something to suit his taste,
from abstruse and recondite theories of mystical
philosophy to anecdotes of a certain kind, which
are told in the plainest terms possible. Although
the work as a whole lacks any comprehensive
plan, the subjects treated in each Book are
logically connected; so many digressions, however, intervene that the most attentive reader
will often lose the thread of the argument. This
is not the place to consider the author's ideas
in detail. He may be called a Pantheist, with the
reservation that at times he uses language in-
consistent with Pantheism and implying belief
in a personal God: he seems to have held the
one and the other view as higher and lower
aspects of the same Truth. The full pantheistic
doctrine is for the spiritually perfect, not for
the self-indulgent who draw immoral inferences

from it. So far as the "swine" are concerned, Jalālu'ddīn, instead of casting his pearls before them, recognises evil and sin as positive facts and asserts that men are the *willing* slaves of passion and therefore responsible for the wickedness they commit. They suffer tribulation and punishment inflicted by Divine justice; yet as His Mercy preceded His Wrath in the beginning, so shall it prevail in the end. The moral and mystical teaching of the *Mathnawī* is centred in Love. If even an earthly love can purify the soul, how much greater must be the power of the Love that leaves "nothing of myself in me"! By developing this principle the poet shows that all partial evil is universal good; that the antithesis of freedom and necessity disappears in harmony of will; and that a religious faith resting on conventional beliefs or intellectual evidences has no value whatever.

Allegory, the hard-worked handmaid of Mysticism, can claim Sūfī literature as her capital province, in which all her features—sublime, exquisite, fantastic, and grotesque—are represented on the most imposing scale. Though much of the symbolism may be found elsewhere, a great deal is peculiar and unique, so that the writings in which it occurs seldom impart their real significance except to those who possess the key to the cipher, while the uninitiated will either understand them literally or not at all. But allegory may also be employed, in the form of fables, anecdotes, apologues, and parables, for the purpose of exposition and illustration; and here it serves, not as a mask or secret code, but as a means of teaching moral and mystical truths by leading the disciple through the familiar to the strange, through the seen to the unseen, through the letter to the spirit.

IV

Following, or rather adapting to his own needs, a method long established in Sūfī poetry, Jalālu'ddīn sets the matter of his discourse within a framework of Tales, which introduce and exemplify the various topics and are frequently interwoven with explanations of their inner meaning. These explanations in their turn may suggest other Tales, which demand fresh explanations, and so it goes on till the original Tale is concluded, when the same process begins over again. The *Mathnawī* is a grand Story-book. There are several hundreds of stories, comprising specimens in almost every *genre*, and no one can accuse the author of lacking invention or fail to admire the easy power with which he moulds his raw material into whatever shape he will. As might be expected, the largest class consists of legends from the *Qur'ān* and its Commentaries, the Traditions of the Prophet, and the Lives of pre-Mohammedan prophets and Muslim saints. *Kalīla and Dimna*, the Arabic version of the Sanskrit *Pancha-tantra*, supplies numerous Beast Fables, where the

animals play the allegorical parts assigned to
them. Jalālu'ddīn borrows much but owes
little: he makes his own everything that comes
to hand. The First Story in the poem is taken
from Ibn Sīnā (Avicenna); others can be traced
back to Sanā'ī, Nizāmī, and 'Attār; and probably
a large number were contributed by popular
collections of anecdotes like the *Jawāmiʿu l-
Hikāyāt* of 'Awfī. What precisely these literary
sources were, and how far they cover the whole
ground, is a question that has yet to be investi-
gated. It is likely, I think, that some, perhaps
many, of the Tales belong to the miscellaneous
stock of "wandering" stories carried to and fro
by dervishes and other travellers, in which case
the author may have put them into verse from
memory.

The Tales themselves, as distinguished from
the doctrinal exegesis with its accompanying
reflections, exhortations, and arguments, occupy
a comparatively small space. Nor will the reader
find in them what often makes the *Mathnawī*
supreme poetry—lofty and sustained flights of
imagination, or passages in which the fervour
of the poet's eloquence and the fullness and
rapidity of his thought remind one of a fire

leaping forward and kindling itself by the impetus of its flames. But such qualities are not in keeping with narrative, and the Tales have their proper merits. Their direct semi-colloquial style, rising to dignity where the subject requires it, contrasts favourably with the artificial diction of most Persian verse. They abound in lively dialogue, masterly satiric and humorous descriptions of human nature, pictures of life and manners illustrating the outlook not only of medieval Sūfism but of Muslims generally, and lessons of universal application drawn from a wisdom that never plays on the surface without contemplating the hidden depths below. Great poet as he is, Jalālu'ddīn loves Truth more than Art. In his *Odes* the tide of enthusiasm sweeps all moralities before it, in the *Mathnawī* he rubs them in with a persistence which renders selection and abridgment necessary. "Listen to this Story," he says, "for 'tis the very marrow of thy inward state"—*mutato nomine de te fabula narratur;* but, unlike Horace, he does not know when to stop. Even his *jocularia*, some of which are far from edifying, turn themselves into ethical homilies or philosophical discourses. Still, the Tales are worth reading, husk, kernel and all. One feels that the Master enjoyed making them and that his disciples (whom he occasionally rebukes for being impatient to hear the rest of the story) must have enjoyed them too.

V

The following fifty-one Stories are a fair
sample of the *Mathnawi* on the side from which
the best general view of its spirit and character
can be obtained by readers approaching it for
the first time. All these versions except two are
in prose, and are based upon the text and literal
translation already published in the E. J. W.
Gibb Memorial Series as far as the end of the
Fourth Book; they also include a few short
anecdotes from Book V. The force and savour
of the *Mathnawi* would be lost in a paraphrase,
and though I have modified here and there my
complete translation, which is intended for
students, the changes hardly affect its closeness
to the original. I have tried to present the Tales
attractively as well as faithfully. Their variety
and interest become more apparent when they
are arranged without regard to their position
and sequence in the Six Books. Many, especially
the longer ones, need pruning and trimming;
and I decided to lighten them rather than leave
them out altogether. As a rule, the temptation
to give extracts has been resisted. No one likes

unfinished stories; if the Poet sometimes breaks off in the middle, it is because his audience knew the end. Brief notes have been added, supplementing his own remarks on the allegorical sense and explaining allusions to matters with which only Muslims are usually familiar. A curious and interesting commentary might be written on the Tales. There is no room for it here, and in any case it could not commend them to the reader half so well as has been done by letting them speak for themselves.

R. A. N.

I

THE KING AND THE HANDMAIDEN[1]

In olden time there was a King to whom belonged the power temporal and also the power spiritual.

It chanced that one day he rode with his courtiers to the chase.

On the king's highway the King espied a Handmaiden: the soul of the King was enthralled by her.

Forasmuch as the bird, his soul, was fluttering in its cage, he gave money and bought the Handmaiden.

After he had bought her and won to his desire, by Divine destiny she sickened.

The King gathered the physicians together from left and right and said to them, "The life of us both is in your hands.

My life is of no account, but she is the life of my life. I am in pain and wounded: she is my remedy.

[1] Book I, *v.* 36 foll. The allegory is plain enough. The King typifies the rational spirit; the Handmaiden in love with the Goldsmith is the soul enamoured of worldly pleasure; the Physician, who by poisoning the Goldsmith cures the Handmaiden of her passion, is the divinely inspired Saint.

Whoever heals her that is my life will bear
away with him my treasure and pearls, large
and small."

They all answered him, saying, "We will hazard
our lives and summon all our skill and put it
into the common stock.

Each one of us is the Messiah of a multi-
tude:[1] in our hands is a medicine for every
pain."

In their arrogance they did not say, "If God
will"; therefore God showed unto them the
weakness of Man.

The more cures and remedies they applied, the
more did the illness increase, and their need
was not fulfilled.

The sick girl became thin as a hair, while the
eyes of the King flowed with tears of blood,
like a river.

*How it became manifest to the King that the
physicians were unable to cure the Handmaiden,
and how he turned his face towards God and
dreamed of a holy man.*

When the King saw the powerlessness of those
physicians, he ran bare-footed to the mosque.

---

[1] Or, according to the oldest MS., "each one of us is a
learned Messiah." The *Masīh*, of course, is Jesus, who says
in the *Qur'ān*, iii, 43, "*I will heal the blind from birth and
the leper, and I will bring the dead to life by permission of
Allah.*"

He entered the mosque and advanced to the
  mihrāb[1] to pray: the prayer-carpet was bathed
  in the King's tears.
On coming to himself out of the flood of ecstasy
  he opened his lips in goodly praise and laud,
Saying, "O Thou whose least gift is the empire
  of the world, what shall I say? for Thou
  knowest the hidden thing.
O Thou with whom we always take refuge in
  our need, once again we have lost the
  way;
But Thou hast said, 'Albeit I know thy secret,
  nevertheless declare it in thine outward
  act.'"
When from the depths of his soul he raised a
  cry of supplication, the sea of Bounty began
  to surge.
Slumber overtook him in the midst of weeping: he dreamed that an old man appeared
And said, "Good tidings, O King! Thy prayers
  are granted. If to-morrow a stranger come to
  thee, he is from me.
He is the skilled physician: deem him veracious,
  for he is trusty and true.
In his remedy behold absolute magic, in his
  nature behold the might of God!"

---

[1] The niche indicating the direction of Mecca.

The meeting of the King with the divine Physician whose coming had been announced to him in a dream.

When the promised hour arrived and day broke
    and the sun, rising from the east, began to
    burn the stars,
The King was in the belvedere, expecting to see
    that which had been shown mysteriously.
He saw a person excellent and worshipful, a
    sun amidst a shadow,
Coming from afar, like the new moon in slender-
    ness and radiance: he was non-existent,[1]
    though existent in the form of phantasy.
In the stranger's countenance the King dis-
    cerned the phantom which he had beheld in
    his dream.
He himself, instead of the chamberlains, went
    forward to meet his guest from the In-
    visible.
Both were seamen who had learned to swim, the
    souls of both were knit together without
    sewing.
The King said, "Thou wert my Beloved in
    reality, not she; but in this world one action
    arises from another.
O thou who art to me as Mustafā,[2] while I

---

[1] *i.e.* in the material world.
[2] Mohammed.

4

am like unto 'Umar[1]—I will gird my loins to
do thee service."
The King opened his hands and clasped him to
his breast and received him, like love, into
his heart and soul,
And kissed his hand and brow and inquired
concerning his home and journey.
So with many a question he led him to the place
of honour. "At last," he said, "I have found
a treasure by being patient.
O gift from God and defence against trouble,
O thou who art the meaning of 'Patience
is the key to joy,'
O thou whose countenance is the answer to
every question, by thee hard knots are loosed
without discussion.
Thou readest all that is in our hearts, thou
givest a helping hand to everyone whose foot
is in the mire."

*How the King led the Physician to the bedside of
the sick girl, that he might see her condition.*

When that meeting and bounteous spiritual
repast was over, he took his hand and conducted him to the harem.
He rehearsed the tale of the invalid and her
sickness and then seated him beside her.
The Physician observed the colour of her

---

[1] The second Caliph.

5

face and felt her pulse; he heard both the symptoms and the circumstances of her malady.

He said, "None of the remedies which they have applied builds up health; those false physicians have wrought destruction.

They were ignorant of the inward state. I seek refuge with God from that which they devise."

He saw the pain, and the secret became open to him, but he concealed it and did not tell the King.

Her pain was not caused by black or yellow bile: the smell of every firewood appears from the smoke.

From her sore grief he perceived that she was heart-sore; well in body but stricken in heart.

Being in love is made manifest by soreness of heart: there is no sickness like heart-sickness.

The lover's ailment is separate from all other ailments: Love is the astrolabe of divine mysteries.

Whether Love be from this side or from that,[1] in the end it leads us Yonder.

How the Physician demanded of the King to be alone with the Handmaiden for the purpose of discovering her malady.

He said, "O King, make the house empty; send away both kinsfolk and strangers.

[1] *i.e.* earthly or heavenly.

6

Let no one listen in the entrance-halls, that I
may ask certain things of this handmaiden."
The house was left empty, not one inhabitant
remained, nobody save the Physician and the
sick girl.
Very gently he asked, "Where is thy native
town? for the treatment suitable to the people
of each town is different.
And in that town who is related to thee? With
whom hast thou kinship and affinity?"
She disclosed to the Physician many things
touching her home and former masters and
fellow-townsmen,
And he, while listening to her story, continued
to observe her pulse and its beating,
So that, if it throbbed at anyone's name, he
might know who was the object of her desire
in the world.
She told of many a town and many a house, and
still no vein of her quivered nor did her cheek
grow pale.
Her pulse kept its wonted time, unimpaired,
till he asked about sweet Samarcand.
Then it jumped, and her face went red and
pale by turns, for she had been parted from
a man of Samarcand, a Goldsmith.
When the Physician found out this secret from
the sick girl, he perceived the source of that
grief and woe.

7

He asked, "In which quarter of the town does
he dwell?"

"*Sar-i Pul* (Bridge-head)," she replied, "and
Ghātafar Street."

"I know," said he, "what your illness is, and I
will at once display the arts of magic in de-
livering you.

Be glad and care-free and have no fear, for I
will do to you that which rain does to the
meadow.

I will be anxious for you, be not you anxious:
I am kinder to you than a hundred fathers.

Beware! tell not this secret to anyone, not
though the King himself should make much
inquiry.

Let your heart become the grave of your
secret, the sooner will your desire be gained.

When seeds are hidden in the earth, their inward secret becomes the verdure of the
garden."

*How the King sent messengers to Samarcand to
fetch the Goldsmith.*

Then he arose and went to the King and acquainted him with a part of the matter.

"The best plan," said he, "is that we should
bring the man here for the purpose of curing
this malady.

Summon the Goldsmith from that far coun-

try; beguile him with gold and robes of
honour."

The King sent thither two messengers, clever
men and competent and very just.

To Samarcand came the two messengers for
the Goldsmith debonair and wanton,

Saying, "O fine master, perfect in knowledge,
thy perfection is famous in all lands.

Lo, such and such a King hath chosen thee
for thy skill in the goldsmith's craft, because
thou art eminent.

Look now, receive these robes of honour and
gold and silver: when thou comest to the
King, thou wilt be his favourite and boon
companion."

The man saw the much wealth and the many
robes: he was beguiled, he parted from his
town and children.

Blithely he set out on the road, unaware that
the King had formed a design against his life.

He mounted an Arab horse and sped on joy-
ously: he deemed a robe of honour what
really was the price of his blood.

O fool, so willingly with thine own feet to enter
on the journey to thy doom!

In his fancy were dreams of riches, power, and
lordship. Said Azrael,[1] "Go thy way: yes,
thou wilt get them!"

[1] The Angel of Death.

9

Proudly and delicately they conducted him to
the King, that he might burn like a moth on
that candle of Tarāz.[1]

The King beheld him, showed great regard for
him, and entrusted to him the treasure house
full of gold.

Then the Physician said, "O mighty Sultan,
give thy handmaiden to this master,

That she may be happy with him and that
the water of union may quench the fire of
passion."

The King bestowed on him that moon-faced
one and wedded the twain who craved each
other's company.

During the space of six months they satisfied
their desires, till the girl was wholly restored
to health.

Afterwards, he prepared a potion for him, so
that he began to dwindle away.

When because of sickness his beauty remained
not, the soul of the girl remained not in his
deadly toils.

Since he appeared ugly and ill-favoured and
sallow-cheeked, little by little he became
unpleasing to her heart.

Those loves which are for the sake of a colour
are not love: in the end they are a disgrace.

[1] This expression is applied to persons of resplendent
beauty, like the women of Tarāz in Turkistan.

Would that he too had lacked all grace, that
such an evil doom might not have come to
pass upon him!

Blood ran from his eye like a river: his hand-
some face had become an enemy to his life.

The peacock's plumage is its enemy. How many
a king hath been slain by his magnificence!

He said, "I am the muskdeer whose gland
caused the hunter to shed its innocent blood,

Or the fox of the field for which they lay in wait
to cut off its head for the sake of the fur,

Or the elephant whose blood was shed by the
mahout for the sake of the ivory.

He who hath slain me for that which is not
myself,[1] does not he know that my blood
sleepeth not?

To-day the doom is on me, to-morrow it is on
him: how should the blood of one like me
rest unavenged?

Although the wall casts a long shadow, yet at
last the shadow turns back again towards it.

The world is the mountain, and our action the
shout: the echo of the shout comes back to
us."

With these words he gave up the ghost. The
Handmaiden was purged of love and pain,

Because love of the dead is not enduring, for the
dead are never coming back to us;

[1] *i.e.* for my beauty.

11

While love of the living is always fresher than
a bud in the spirit and in the sight.

Choose the love of that Living One, who is
everlasting and gives thee to drink of the
wine that increases life.

Choose the love of Him from whose love all the
prophets gained power and glory.

Do not say, "We have no admission to that
King." Dealings with the generous are not
difficult.

II

THE GROCER AND THE PARROT[1]

THERE was a Grocer who had a parrot, a sweet-
voiced, green, talking parrot.

Perched on the bench, it would watch over the
shop in its master's absence and talk to the
customers.

Once, as it sprang from the bench and flew
away, it spilled some bottles of rose-oil.

Its master came from his house and merchant-
wise seated himself at ease on the bench.

Finding the bench wet with oil and his clothes
greasy, he smote the parrot on the head: it
was made bald by the blow.

For some few days it refrained from speech;
the Grocer, repenting, heaved deep sighs

And tore his beard, saying, "Alas, the sun of
my prosperity is gone under the clouds.

Would that my hand had been paralysed when
I struck such a blow on the head of that
sweet-tongued one!"

He was giving presents to every dervish, that
he might get back the speech of his bird.

---

[1] Book I, *v.* 247. This story illustrates the folly of reason-
ing by analogy (*qiyās*) and judging by appearances.

After three days and nights he was seated on
the bench, distraught and sorrowful like a
man in despair,

Showing the bird all sorts of marvels, that perchance it might begin to speak,

When a bare-headed dervish passed by, clad in
a *jawlaq*, his head hairless as the outside of a
bowl.

Thereupon the parrot began to talk, screeched
at the dervish, and said, "Hey, fellow!

How were you mixed up with the bald, O bald-
pate? Did you, then, spill oil from a bottle?"

The bystanders laughed at the parrot's infer-
ence, because it deemed the wearer of the
frock to be like itself.

III

THE MAN WHO FLEW TO HINDUSTĀN[1]

ONE morn, to Solomon in his hall of justice
A noble suitor came, running in haste,
His countenance pale with anguish, his lips blue.
"What ails thee, Khwāja?" asked the King.
  Then he:
"'Twas Azrael—ah, such a look he cast
On me of rage and vengeance." "Come now, ask
What boon thou wilt." "Protector of our lives,
I pray thee, bid the Wind convey me straight
To Hindustān: thy servant, there arrived,
Shall peradventure save his soul from Death."

How folk do ever flee from dervishhood
Into the jaws of greed and idle hope!
Your fear of dervishhood is that doomed man's
  terror,
Greed and ambition are your Hindustān.

Solomon bade the Wind convey him swiftly
Over the sea to farthest Hindustān.
On the morrow, when the King in audience
  sate,

[1] Book I, v. 956.

15

He said to Azrael, "Wherefore didst thou look
Upon that Musulmān so wrathfully,
His home knew him no more?" "Nay, not in
  wrath,"
Replied the Angel, "did I look on him;
But seeing him pass by, I stared in wonder,
For God had bidden me take his soul that day
In Hindustān. I stood there marvelling.
Methought, even if he had a hundred wings,
'Twere far for him to fly to Hindustān."

Judge all things of the world by this same rule
And ope your eyes and see! Away from whom
Shall we run headlong? From ourselves?
  Absurd!
Whom take ourselves away from? God? O
  crime!

IV

THE SŪFĪ AND THE UNFAITHFUL SERVANT[1]

ONE night a wandering Sūfī became a guest at a monastery for dervishes.

He tied his ass in the stable; then he joined the brethren on the dais,

Who were engaged in devotional meditation: the friend of God is a better companion than a book.

The Sūfī's book does not consist of ink and letters: it is naught but a heart white as snow.

When at last the meditation of those godly Sūfīs came to an end in ecstasy and enthusiasm

They furnished the guest with food, and he then bethought him of his ass.

He said to the servant, "Go into the stable and provide straw and barley for the beast."

"God help us!"[2] he replied, "why talk too much? This has been my job for ever so long."

[1] Book II, v. 156. The Unfaithful Servant represents the Devil and the religious hypocrite.

[2] *Lā hawl*, "there is no power (or strength except in God Almighty)."

17

The Sūfī said, "First wet the barley, for 'tis an old ass, and his teeth are shaky."

"God help us!" said he. "Why are you telling this to me, Sir? I am the one to give instructions."

The Sūfī said, "After having taken off his saddle put the *manbal* salve on his sore back."

"God help us!" exclaimed the servant. "Why, O purveyor of wisdom, I have had a thousand guests of your sort,

And all have departed from us well pleased: our guests are dear to us as our kinsfolk and as life itself."

The Sūfī said, "Give him water, but let it be lukewarm." "God help us!" cried the other. "I am ashamed of you."

The Sūfī said, "Put a little straw in his barley." "God help us! Cut short this palaver," he replied.

The Sūfī said, "Sweep his place clear of stones and dung, and if it is damp, sprinkle some dry earth on it."

"God help us!" cried he. "Implore God's help, O father, and don't waste words on a messenger who knows his business."

The Sūfī said, "Take the comb and curry his back." "God help us! Do have some shame, O father," said he.

Then, briskly girding up his loins, "I go,"

said he; "first I will fetch the straw and barley."

Off he went and never gave a thought to the stable: he beguiled the Sūfī with the sleep of the hare.[1]

The servant went off to some rascally friends and made a mockery of the Sūfī's admonition.

The Sūfī was fatigued by his journey and lay down: with eyes closed he was dreaming

That his ass had fallen into the clutch of a wolf which was tearing its back and thighs.

"God help us!" he exclaimed. "What melancholy madness is this? Oh, where is that kindly servant?"

Again, he would see his ass going along the road and tumbling now into a well and now into a ditch.

He was dreaming unpleasant dreams, he was reciting the *Fātiha*[2] and the *Qāri'a*.[3]

He asked himself, "What can be done? My friends have hurried out and left all the doors locked."

Again he would say, "Oh, I wonder—that wretched servant! Did not he partake of bread and salt with us?

---

[1] *i.e.* he caused the Sūfī to imagine that he (the Servant) was wide-awake and attentive, though he was really like the hare, which sleeps with its eyes open.

[2] The opening chapter of the *Qur'ān*.

[3] The hundred-and-first chapter of the *Qur'ān*.

19

I showed him nothing but courtesy: why should
he behave despitefully to me?

There must be a cause for every hatred; our
common humanity inspires feelings of friendship."

But then he would think, "When did Adam,
the kind and generous, do an injury to
Iblis?[1]

What was done by man to snake and scorpion
that they seek to inflict death and pain upon
him?

To rend is the instinct of the wolf: after all,
envy is conspicuous in mankind."

Again he would say, "It is wrong to think evil:
why should I bear such thoughts against my
brother?"

But then he would reflect that prudence consists in thinking evil: how shall he that thinks
no evil remain unhurt?

So deep was the Sūfī's anxiety, and meanwhile
his ass was in such a plight that—may it
befall our enemies!

The poor ass lay amidst earth and stones, with
his saddle awry and his halter torn,

Wellnigh killed by fatigue, without fodder all
the night long, now at the last gasp and now
perishing.

All night the ass was repeating, "O God, I give

[1] Satan. The word is a corruption of $\delta\iota\acute{a}\beta o\lambda o\varsigma$.

up the barley, but am I not to have even a handful of straw?"

With mute eloquence he was saying, "O Shaykhs, have pity, for I am consumed with anguish because of this rude, impudent rogue."

All night till dawn the miserable ass rolled on his side, tormented by hunger.

At daybreak the servant came and instantly set the saddle straight on his back,

And after the fashion of ass-dealers gave him two or three blows with a goad: he did to the ass what suited a cur like him.

The sharp pricks made the ass jump up—hath an ass speech to describe his feelings?

When the Sūfī mounted him and got going, the ass began to fall on his face again and again,

And the travellers lifted him up every time: they all thought something was wrong.

One would twist his ears hard, while another sought for the laceration under his palate,

And another searched for the stone in his shoe, and another looked for the dirt in his eye.

"O Shaykh," they asked, "what is the cause of this? Didn't you say yesterday, 'Thank God, the ass is in fine fettle'?"

The Sūfī replied, "The ass that lived all night

on 'God help us!' cannot get along except in this manner.

Since his only food was 'God help us' he was praying to God by night and is prostrating himself by day."

V

THE FALCON AMONGST THE OWLS[1]

THE Falcon is he that comes back to the King.
He that has lost the way is the blind falcon.

It lost the way and fell into the wilderness;[2]
then in the wilderness it fell amongst owls.[3]

The Falcon is wholly light emanating from the
Light of Divine Grace, but Destiny hath
blinded it,

Thrown dust in its eyes and led it far from the
right way and left it amongst the owls in the
wilderness.

To crown all, the owls attack it and tear its
lovely wing-feathers and plumes.

A clamour arose amongst the owls—"Ha! the
Falcon hath come to seize our dwelling-
place."[4]

'Twas as when the street-dogs, wrathful and
terrifying, have fallen upon the frock of a
strange dervish.

[1] Book II, v. 1131. The Falcon is a type of the righteous
man, and particularly the prophet or saint, whose heart is
turned to God.
[2] The world.
[3] Worldlings.
[4] The unbelievers asserted that the prophets were seeking
power and wealth for themselves.

"How am I fit," says the Falcon, "to consort
with owls? I give up to the owls a hundred
wildernesses like this.

I do not wish to stay here, I am going, I will
return to the King of kings.

O ye owls, do not kill yourselves with agitation!
I am not settling here, I am going home.

This ruin seems a thriving abode to you, but
my pleasure-seat is the King's wrist."

"Beware," said the great Owl to his friends,
"the Falcon is plotting to uproot you from
house and home.

He will seize our houses by his cunning, he
will then turn us out of our nests by his
hypocrisy.

He boasts of the King and the King's wrist in
order that he may lead us astray, simpletons
as we are!

How should a petty bird be familiar with the
King? Do not hearken to him, if ye have any
understanding.

As for his saying, from deceit and feint and
artifice, 'The King with all his retinue is
searching after me,'

Here's an absurd mad fancy for you, here's a
vain brag and a snare to catch blockheads!

If the smallest owl strike at his brain, where is
succour for him from the King?"

The Falcon said, "If a single feather of mine

be broken, the King of kings will uproot the whole owlery.

An owl forsooth! Even if a falcon vex my heart and maltreat me,

The King will heap up in every hill and dale hundreds of thousands of stacks of falcons' heads.

His favour keeps watch over me: wherever I go, the King is following behind.

My image is abiding in the King's heart: sick would the King be without my image.

When the King bids me fly in His Way, I soar up to the heart's zenith, like His beams.

I fly as a moon and sun, I rend the curtains of the skies.

O blest is the owl that had the good fortune to apprehend my mystery!

Cling to me, that ye may rejoice and may become royal falcons, although ye are but owls.

I am the owner of the spiritual kingdom, I am not a lickspittle. The King is beating the falcon-drum for me from Beyond.

My falcon-drum is the call, '*Return!*'[1] God is my witness in despite of adversary.

I am not a congener of the King of kings—far be it from Him!—but I have light from His radiance.

[1] *Qur'ān*, lxxxix, 27-28. "*O soul at peace, return to thy Lord, well pleased and well pleased with!*"

25

Since my *genus* is not the *genus* of my King, my
ego has passed away for the sake of His ego.
My ego has passed away, He remains alone: I
roll at the feet of His horse like the dust.
My individual self became dust, and the only
trace of it is the print of His feet upon its
dust.
Become dust at His feet for the sake of that
footprint, in order that ye may be as the
diadem on the head of the exalted.
Let not my puny form deceive you. Partake of
my banquet ere I depart."

VI

THE MAN WHO FANCIED HE SAW THE NEW MOON[1]

ONCE, in 'Umar's time, when the Month of
Fast came round, some people ran to the top
of a hill,
In order to have the luck of seeing the new
moon;[2] and one of them said, "Look, there
is the new moon, O 'Umar!"
As 'Umar did not see the moon in the sky, he said,
"This moon has risen from thy imagination.
Otherwise, since I am a better observer of the
heavens than thou art, how do I not see the
pure crescent?
Wet thy hand and rub it on thine eyebrow, and
then look for the new moon."

[1] Book II, v. 112.
[2] "The night on which Ramadān (the month of abstinence, the ninth month of the year) is expected to commence
is called 'Leylet er-Rooyeh,' or the Night of the Observation
[of the new moon]. In the afternoon, or earlier, during the
preceding day, several persons are sent a few miles into the
desert, where the air is particularly clear, in order to obtain
a sight of the new moon: for the fast commences on the
next day after the new moon has been seen. . . . The evidence of one Muslim, that he has seen the new moon, is
sufficient for the proclaiming of the fast." Lane, *The Modern
Egyptians*, ch. xxv.

27

When the man wetted his eyebrow, he could not see the moon. "O King," said he, "there is no moon; it has disappeared."

"Yes," said 'Umar, "the hair of thine eyebrow became a bow and shot at thee an arrow of false opinion."

One crooked hair had misled him, so that he vainly boasted to have seen the moon.

Inasmuch as a crooked hair veils the sky, how will it be if all your members are crooked?

Straighten your members by the help of the righteous. O you who would go straight, turn not aside from the door where the righteous dwell.

VII

THE BRAGGART AND THE SHEEP'S TAIL[1]

A PERSON, who on account of his poverty was lightly esteemed, used to grease his moustache every morning with the skin of a fat sheep's tail,

And go amongst the rich, saying, "I was at the party and had a good dinner."

He would gaily touch his moustache, meaning, "Look at it!

For it bears witness to the truth of my words, and is the token of my having eaten greasy and delicious food."

His belly would say in mute response, "May God confound the plots of the liars!

Thy boasting hath set me on fire: may thy greasy moustache be torn out!

Beggar that thou art! Were it not for thy foul bluster, some generous man would have taken pity on me.

If thou hadst shown the ailment and hadst not played false, some physician would have devised a remedy for it."

[1] Book III, *v.* 732.

29

His belly pleaded against his moustache and
 secretly had recourse to prayer,
Crying, "O God, expose this idle brag of the
 base, in order that the noble may be moved
 with pity towards me."
The belly's prayer was answered: the ardency
 of need produced a flame.[1]
God hath said, "Though thou be a profligate
 and idolater, I will answer when Thou callest
 Me."
Do thou cleave unto prayer and ever cry out:
 in the end it will deliver thee from the hands
 of the ghoul.
When the belly committed itself to God, the
 cat came and carried off the sheep's tail.
They pursued her, but she escaped. The brag-
 gart's child turned pale in fear of a scolding;
Nevertheless that little boy came into the midst
 of the company and destroyed his father's
 prestige.
"Father," said he, "the sheep's tail, with which
 you grease your lips and moustache every
 morning—
The cat came and suddenly snatched it away.
 I ran hard, but it was no use."
Those who were present laughed in astonishment, and their feelings of compassion were
 roused.

[1] Literally, "put forth a flag."

30

They invited him to eat and kept him well fed,
   they sowed the seed of pity in his soil;
And he, having tasted honesty from the noble,
   became humbly devoted to honesty.

VIII

THE THREE FISHES[1]

THIS, O obstinate man, is the story of the lake
in which there were three great fishes.

You will have read it in *Kalīla*,[2] but that is only
the husk of the story, while this is the spiritual
kernel.

Some fishermen passed by the lake and saw the
concealed prey.

They hastened to bring the net: the fishes
observed them and understood their inten-
tion.

The intelligent fish[3] resolved to migrate, he
resolved to make the difficult unwelcome
journey.

He said, "I will not consult these others, for
they will certainly weaken the strength of my
purpose.

Love for their native place holds sway over
their souls: their indolence and ignorance
will affect me too."

---

[1] Book IV, *v.* 2202.
[2] *Kalīla and Dimna*, the Arabic version of the Sanskrit
Pancha-tantra, made by Ibn al-Muqaffa' in the eighth century A.D.
[3] The Sūfī whose object is union with God.

For consultation, a goodly and spiritually living
    person is needed, so that he may endow thee
    with spiritual life; and where is that living one
    to be found?

O traveller, take counsel with a traveller, for a
    woman's counsel will make thy foot lame.

Pass beyond "love of country," do not stop at
    its outward sense. O soul, thy real country is
    Yonder, not here.

If thou desire thy country, cross to the other
    bank of the river. Do not misread the true
    Tradition of the Prophet.[1]

The wary fish swam away on his breast: he was
    going from his perilous abode towards the
    Sea of Light,

Like the deer which is pursued by a dog and
    keeps running so long as there is a single
    nerve in its body.

Hare's sleep[2] with the dog in pursuit is a sin;
    how indeed should sleep dwell in the eyes of
    him who hath fear?

That fish departed and took the way to the Sea:
    he chose the far way and illimitable expanse.

The second fish[3] said in the hour of tribulation,

    [1] "Love of country is part of the Faith."
    [2] The real heedlessness and indifference of one who super-
ficially has the appearance of being on his guard.
    [3] A symbol of those who, lacking the perfect wisdom of
the prophet or saint, are wise enough to attach themselves
to a spiritual Guide and follow him on the Way to Salvation.

when he was left without the protection of the intelligent one,

"He is gone to the Sea and is freed from sorrow: my good comrade is lost to me.

But I will not think of that. Now I must attend to myself. Let me feign to be dead

And turn my belly upwards and my back downwards and float on the water.

I will become dead, I will commit myself to the water: to die before death[1] is to be safe from torment."

To die before death is to be safe, O youth: even so hath Mustafá[2] commanded us,

Who said, "Die, all of you, ere death come; else ye will die in grievous affliction."

The second fish died in that manner and threw his belly upwards: the water was carrying him, now alow, now aloft.

The fishermen were exceedingly vexed and cried, "Alas, the best fish is dead."

He rejoiced at their saying "Alas"; he thought to himself, "My trick has come off, I am delivered from the sword."

A worthy fisherman seized him and spat on him and flung him to the ground.

Then the half-wise fish, rolling over and over, slipped quietly into the water. Meanwhile

[1] The mystical death to self (*fanā*).
[2] Mohammed.

the foolish one[1] was darting to and fro in agitation.

That simpleton kept leaping about, right and left, in order that he might save his skin by his own efforts.

They cast the net, and he was caught in the net: his foolishness ensconced him in the fire of perdition.

On the top of the fire, on the surface of a frying-pan, he became the bedfellow of Folly.

There he was seething in the flames, while Reason asked, *"Did not a Warner come to thee?"*[2]

He, from the rack of torture and tribulation, was replying, like the souls of the unbelievers: *they said, "Yea."*

---

[1] The carnal man who has no light of his own and will not submit to be led by that of another.

[2] As the infidels shall be asked by the keepers of Hell on the Day of Judgment (*Qur'ān*, lxvii, 8).

IX

THE GREEK AND CHINESE ARTISTS[1]

THE Chinese said, "We have the greater skill";
the Greeks said, "The superior excellence
belongs to us."

"I will put you both to the test," said the Sultan, "and see which party makes good its
claim."

There were two rooms with door facing
door: the Chinese took one, the Greeks the
other.

The Chinese asked the Sultan for a hundred
colours: he opened his treasury that they
might receive them,

And every morning, by his bounty, the colours
were dispensed to the Chinese.

The Greeks said, "For our work no colours
are necessary: we need only remove the
rust."

They shut the door and began to burnish:
the walls became bright and pure like the
sky.

There is a way from many-colouredness to

[1] Book I, v. 3467.

colourlessness: colour is the cloud, colourlessness the moon.[1]

Whatsoever light and splendour you see in the
clouds, know that it comes from the stars and
the moon and the sun.

When the Chinese finished their work, they
beat drums in jubilation.

The Sultan entered and looked at the pictures:
their beauty almost robbed him of understanding.

Afterwards he visited the Greeks. They had
lifted the curtain between themselves and
the Chinese,

So that the Chinese paintings were reflected
upon those shining walls.

All that he had seen there seemed more beautiful here: 'twas drawing the eye from the
socket.

The Greeks, O father, are the Sūfīs. They are
without learning and books and erudition,

But they have burnished their hearts and
made them pure of greed and avarice and
hatred.

That pure mirror[2] is, beyond doubt, the heart
which receives images innumerable.

[1] Cf. Shelley's—
"Life, like a dome of many-coloured glass,
Stains the white radiance of eternity."
[2] *i.e.* the walls which the Greeks had polished.

The spiritual Moses[1] holds in his bosom the
infinite form of the Unseen reflected from
the mirror of his heart.[2]

---

[1] The illumined saint. There is an allusion to the command given to Moses on Mt. Sinai (*Qur'ān*, xxvii, 12;
xxviii, 32), "*Thrust thy hand into thy bosom: it will come
forth white without hurt.*"

[2] The Perfect Man is a microcosm in which all the divine
attributes are reflected as in a mirror.

X

THE DRUGGIST AND THE
CLAY-EATER[1]

A CLAY-EATER went to a druggist to buy a quantity of fine hard sugar-loaf.

The druggist, who was a crafty, vigilant man, informed his customer that the balance-weight was clay.[2]

"I want the sugar at once," replied the clay-eater; "let the weight be what you will."

He said to himself, "What does it matter to me? Clay is better than gold."

The druggist therefore put the clay, which he had ready, in one scale of the balance,

And began to break with his hand the equivalent amount of sugar for the other scale.

Since he had no pick-axe, he took a long time and kept the customer waiting.

Whilst he was busy with the sugar, the clay-

---

[1] Book IV, *v.* 625. The practice of geophagy is often mentioned in the *Mathnawī*. According to Schlimmer (*Terminologie médico-pharmaceutique*, Teheran, 1874, p. 299) it is common amongst Persian women. The province of Khurāsān gave its name to a brilliant white clay, which was eaten roasted; and there were other well-known varieties.

[2] Implying that it was deficient.

eater, unable to restrain his appetite, helped himself covertly to the clay,

In a terrible fright lest the druggist's eye should fall upon him of a sudden for the purpose of testing his honesty.

The druggist saw him but feigned to be busy, saying to himself, "Come, take some more, O pale-face.

If you will be a thief and filch my clay, go on, for you are eating out of your own side.

You are afraid of me, because you are a stupid ass; I am only afraid that you will eat too little.

Busy as I am, I am not such a fool as to let you get too much of my sugar.

When you see the amount of sugar you have bought, then you will know who was foolish and careless."

XI

THE FROZEN SNAKE[1]

A SNAKE-CATCHER went to the mountains to catch a snake by his incantations.

Whether one be slow or quick, he that is a seeker will be a finder.

Always apply yourself with both hands to seeking, for search is an excellent guide on the way.

Though you be lame and limping and bent in figure and unmannerly, ever creep towards God and be in quest of Him.

Now by speech, now by silence, and now by smelling, catch in every quarter the scent of the King.

Smell all the way from the part to the Whole, O noble one; smell all the way from opposite to opposite, O wise one.

Assuredly wars bring peace; the snake-catcher sought the snake for the purpose of friendship.

Man seeks a snake for his friend and cares for one that is without care for him.[2]

[1] Book III, v. 976.
[2] The snake, as the poet explains afterwards, is the sensual "self," which is Man's worst enemy.

The snake-catcher was searching in the mountains for a big snake in the days of snow.

He espied there a huge dead serpent, at the aspect whereof his heart was filled with fear.

The snake-catcher catches snakes in order to astonish the people—oh, the foolishness of the people!

Man is a mountain:[1] how should he be led into temptation? How should a mountain be astonished by a snake?

Wretched Man does not know himself: he has come from a high estate and fallen into lowlihood.

Man has sold himself cheaply: he was satin, he has patched himself on to a tattered cloak.

Hundreds of thousands of snakes and mountains are amazed at him: how, then, has he become amazed and in love with a snake?

The snake-catcher took up the serpent and came to Baghdād in order to excite astonishment.

For the sake of a paltry fee he carried along with him a serpent like the pillar of a house,

Saying, "I have brought a dead serpent: I have suffered agonies in hunting it."

He thought it was dead, but it was alive, and he had not inspected it very well.

---

[1] Man, created in the image of God, resembles a mountain in the grandeur and might of his essential nature.

It was frozen by frosts and snow; it was living, though it presented the appearance of the dead.

The World is frozen: its name is *jamād* (inanimate); *jāmid* means "frozen," O master.

Wait till the Sun of the Resurrection shall rise, that thou mayst see the movement of the World's body!

At last the would-be showman arrived at Baghdād, to set up a public show at the crossroads.

The man set up a show on the bank of the Tigris, and a great hubbub arose in the city—

"A snake-catcher has brought a serpent; he has captured a marvellous rare beast."

Myriads of simpletons assembled, who had become a prey to him as he to his folly.

They were waiting to see the serpent, and he too waited for them to assemble.

The greater the crowd, the better goes the begging and contributing of money.

Myriads of idle babblers gathered round, forming a ring, sole against sole.[1]

Men took no heed of women: all were mingled in the throng, like nobles and common folk at the Resurrection.

When he began to lift the cloth covering the serpent, the people strained their necks,

[1] *i.e.* standing closely packed together on tiptoe.

43

And saw that the serpent, which had been
frozen by intense cold, lay underneath a
hundred coarse woollen blankets and coverlets.

He had bound it with thick ropes: the careful
keeper had taken great precautions.

During the interval of expectation and coming
together, the sun of 'Irāq shone upon the
snake.

The sun of the hot country warmed it: the cold
humours went out of its limbs.

It was dead, and it revived: the astonished serpent began to uncoil itself.

By the stirring of the dead serpent the people's
amazement was increased a hundred thou-
sandfold.

They fled, shrieking, while the cords binding the
serpent went crack, crack, one after another.

It burst the bonds and glided out from beneath
—a hideous dragon roaring like a lion.

Multitudes were killed in the rout: a hundred
heaps were made of the fallen slain.

The snake-catcher stood paralysed with fear,
crying, "What have I brought from the mountains and the desert?"

The blind sheep awakened the wolf and un-
wittingly went to meet its Azrael.

The serpent made one mouthful of that dolt:
blood-drinking is easy for a Hajjāj.

44

It wound itself on a pillar and crunched the bones of the devoured man.

The serpent is thy carnal soul: how is it dead? It is only frozen by grief and lack of means.
If it obtain the means of Pharaoh, by whose command the Nile would flow,
Then it will begin to act like Pharaoh and waylay a hundred such as Moses and Aaron.
That serpent, under stress of poverty, is a little worm; but a gnat is made a falcon by power and riches.
Keep the serpent in the snow of separation from its desires. Beware, do not carry it into the sun of 'Irāq!

XII

THE SINCERE PENITENT[1]

A MAN was going to attend the Friday prayers:
he saw the people leaving the mosque

And asked one of them why they were depart-
ing so early.

He replied, "The Prophet has prayed with the
congregation and finished his worship.

How art thou going in, O foolish person, after
the Prophet has given the blessing?"

"Alas!" he cried; and it seemed as though the
smell of his heart's blood issued, like smoke,
from that burning sigh.

One of the congregation said, "Give me this
sigh, and all my prayers are thine."

He answered, "I give thee the sigh and accept
thy prayers." The other took the sigh that
was so full of regret and longing.

At night, whilst he was asleep, a Voice said to
him, "Thou hast bought the Water of Life
and Salvation.

For the sake of that which thou hast chosen,
the prayers of all the people have been accepted."

[1] Book II, *v.* 2771.

46

XIII

THE PALADIN OF QAZWĪN[1]

Now hear a pleasant tale—and mark the scene—
About the way and custom of Qazwīn,
Where barbers ply their needles to tattoo
Folk's arms and shoulders with designs in blue.

Once a Qazwīnī spoke the barber fair:
"Tattoo me, please; make something choice
    and rare."
"What figure shall I paint, O paladin?"
"A furious lion: punch him boldly in.
Leo is my ascendant: come, tattoo
A lion, and let him have his fill of blue."
"On what place must I prick the deft design?"
"Trace it upon my shoulder, line by line."
He took the needle and dabbed and dabbed it
    in.
Feeling his shoulder smart, the paladin
Began to yell—"You have killed me quite, I
    vow:
What is this pattern you are doing now?"
"Why, sir, a lion, as you ordered me."
"Commencing with what limb?" demanded he.

[1] Book I, v. 2981.

47

"His tail," was the reply. "O best of men,
Leave out the tail, I beg, and start again.
The lion's tail and rump chokes me to death;
It's stuck fast in my windpipe, stops my
    breath.
O lion-maker, let him have no tail,
Or under these sharp stabs my heart will
    fail."
Another spot the barber 'gan tattoo,
Without fear, without favour, without rue.
"Oh, oh! which part of him is this? Oh
    dear!"
"This," said the barber, "is your lion's ear."
"Pray, doctor, not an ear of any sort!
Leave out his ears and cut the business short."
The artist quickly set to work once more:
Again our hero raised a doleful roar.
"On which third limb now is the needle em-
    ployed?"
"His belly, my dear sir." "Hold, hold!" he
    cried.
"Perish the lion's belly, root and branch!
How should the glutted lion want a paunch?"
Long stood the barber there in mute dismay,
His finger 'twixt his teeth; then flung away
The needle, crying, "All the wide world o'er
Has such a thing e'er happened heretofore?
Why, God Himself did never make, I tell ye,
A lion without tail or ears or belly!"

MORAL

Brother, endure the pain with patience fresh,
To gain deliverance from the miscreant flesh.
Whoso is freed from selfhood's vain conceit,
Sky, sun and moon fall down to worship at his
  feet.

XIV

THE GREEDY INSOLVENT[1]

THERE was an Insolvent without house or
home, who remained in prison and pitiless
bondage.

He would unconscionably eat the rations of the
prisoners; on account of his appetite he lay
heavy as Mt. Qāf[2] on the hearts of the people
in the gaol.

No one durst eat a mouthful of bread, because
that food-snatcher would carry off his entire
meal.

The prisoners came to complain to the
Cadi's agent, who was possessed of discern-
ment,

Saying, "Take our salutations to the Cadi and
relate to him the sufferings inflicted on us
by this vile man;

For he is never out of prison, and he is a vaga-
bond, a lickspittle, and a nuisance.

Like a fly, he impudently presents himself at
every meal without invitation or salaam.

---

[1] Book II, v. 585.
[2] The inaccessible range of mountains by which, according
to Muslim belief, the earth is surrounded.

To him the food of sixty persons is nothing; he
pretends to be deaf if you say 'Enough!'

Not a morsel reaches the ordinary prisoner,
or if by a hundred shifts he discover some
food,

That hell-throat at once comes forward with the
argument that God has said, '*Eat ye.*'[1]

Justice, justice against such a three years'
famine! May the shadow of our lord endure
for ever!

Either let this buffalo out of prison, or make
him a regular allowance of food from a trust-
fund.

O thou by whom men and women are made
happy, do justice! Thy help is invoked and
besought."

The courteous agent went to the Cadi and
related the complaint to him point by
point.

The Cadi summoned the Insolvent to his presence, and inquired about him from his own
officers.

All the complaints which the prisoners had set
forth were proved to the Cadi.

The Cadi said to him, "Get up and depart from
this prison: go to the house that belongs to
you by inheritance."

[1] *Qur'ān*, vii, 29.

He replied, "My house and home consist in
thy bounty; as in the case of an infidel, thy
prison is my Paradise.[1]

If thou drive me from the prison and turn me
out, I shall certainly die of beggary and destitution."

He pleaded like the Devil, who said, "*O
Lord, grant me a respite till the Day of Resurrection,*[2]

For 'tis my pleasure to be in the prison of this
World, so that I may slay the children of mine
Enemy,

And, if anyone have some food of Faith and a
single loaf as provision for the journey to the
Life hereafter,

I may seize it by guile and cunning, and
they in sorrow may raise an outcry of
lamentation,

While sometimes I threaten them with poverty,
and sometimes bind their eyes with the spell
of tress and mole."

The Cadi said, "Prove that you are insolvent."
"Here are the prisoners," he replied, "as my
witnesses."

---

[1] The Prophet is reported to have said, "This world is the
infidel's Paradise."

[2] *Qur'ān*, vii, 13, slightly altered.

"They," said the Cadi, "are suspect, because
they are fleeing from you and weeping blood
on account of you;

They are suing for deliverance from you: by
reason of self-interest their testimony is
worthless."

All the people of the court said, "We bear
witness both to his insolvency and his moral
degeneracy."

Everyone whom the Cadi questioned about his
condition said, "My lord, wash thy hands of
this Insolvent."

Then said the Cadi, "March him round the city
for all to see, and cry, 'This man is an insolvent and a great rogue.

Let no one sell to him on credit, let no one lend
him a farthing.

Whatever charge of fraud may be brought
against him, I will not commit him to prison in
future.[1]

His insolvency has been proven to me: he
possesses nothing, neither money nor goods.'"

When the show[2] started, they brought along the
camel of a Kurd who sold firewood.

He made a great row, but all in vain, though he

---

[1] According to Muslim law, a debtor whose insolvency
has been proven is not liable to imprisonment.

[2] *i.e.* the preparations for parading the Insolvent.

conciliated the police officer with the gift of
a *dāng*.[1]

Upon the camel was seated that sore famine,[2]
while the owner ran at its heels.

They sped from quarter to quarter and from
street to street, till the whole town knew him
by sight.

Ten loud-voiced criers, Turks and Kurds and
Greeks and Arabs, made the following pro-
clamation:

"This man is insolvent and has nothing: let no
one lend him a brass farthing;

He does not possess a single mite, patent or
latent; he is a bankrupt, a piece of falsehood,
a cunning knave, an oil-bag.

Beware! Beware! Have no dealings with him:
when he brings the ox to sell, tie up your
money;

And if ye bring this decayed wretch for judgement, I will not imprison a corpse."

At nightfall, when the Insolvent dismounted,
the Kurd said to him, "I live a long way off.

You have been riding on my camel since morning. Never mind the barley,[3] but at least give
me what will pay for the straw."

---

[1] About a farthing.
[2] The Insolvent.
[3] *i.e.* "I don't ask you to pay me in full."

"Why," he rejoined, "what were we doing all
day? Where are your wits? Is none of them
at home?

My insolvency has been drummed up to the
Seventh Heaven, but you have not heard the
bad news!

Your ears were filled with foolish hope. Such
hope makes one deaf and blind, my lad."

XV

JOSEPH AND HIS GUEST[1]

THE loving friend came from the ends of the
earth and became the guest of Joseph the
truthful;

For they had been friends in childhood, reclining together on the cushion of acquaint-
ance.

He spoke of the injustice and envy of Joseph's
brethren. Joseph said, "That was a chain,
and I was the lion.

The lion is not disgraced by the chain: I do not
complain of God's decree."

After Joseph had told him his story, he said,
"Now, O such and such, what traveller's gift
hast thou brought for me?

Come, produce it." At this demand the guest
sobbed aloud in confusion.

"How many a gift," he said, "did I seek for
thee! but no worthy gift came into my
sight.

How should I bring a grain of gold to the mine?
How should I bring a drop of water to the
sea?

[1] Book I, *v.* 3157.

56

I should only bring cumin to Kirmān[1] if I
brought my heart and soul as a gift to thee.

There is no grain that is not in this barn except
thy incomparable beauty.

I deemed it fitting that I should bring to thee a
mirror like the inward light of a pure heart,

That thou mayst behold thy beauteous face
therein, O thou who, like the sun, art the
lamp of heaven.

I have brought thee a mirror, O light of mine
eyes, so that when thou seest thy face thou
mayst think of me."

[1] To "bring cumin to Kirmān" (in Southern Persia)
means the same thing as "carrying coals to Newcastle."

XVI

THE MAN WHO TRUSTED THE BEAR[1]

A Dragon was pulling a Bear into its jaws: a
    valiant man went and succoured it.

When it was delivered from the Dragon, it
    followed its benefactor like the dog of the
    Seven Sleepers.[2]

He, being fatigued, lay down to rest: the Bear,
    from devotion to him, became his guard.

A holy man passed by and said to him, "What
    is the matter? What has this Bear to do with
    thee, O brother?"

He related his adventure with the Dragon.
    "Fool!" said the other, "do not set thy heart
    on a bear."

The man thought to himself, "He is envious";
    then he said aloud, "See how fond of me it is!"

"The fondness of fools is deceiving," he replied;
    "my envy is better for thee than its affection.

[1] Book II, *v.* 1932.

[2] The *Qur'ān*, ch. xviii, relates the legend of the seven
Christian youths of Ephesus who, in the reign of the Emperor Decius, fled from persecution and took refuge in a
cave, where they slept for three hundred and nine years.
The dog which accompanied them (*vv.* 17 and 21) is said by
some to have had the name *ar-Raqīm* (*v.* 8); but this identi-
fication is very doubtful.

Drive the Bear away and come with me, do not
make friends with the Bear, do not forsake
one of thy own kind.

I am not less than a bear, O noble sir: abandon
it in order that I may be thy comrade.

My heart is trembling for thee: do not go into
a forest with a bear like this.

My heart has never trembled in vain; this is
the Light of God, not pretence or idle
boasting.

I am the true believer who sees by the Light of
God.[1] Beware, beware! Flee from this fire-
temple!"[2]

He said all this, but it entered not into his ear.
Suspicion is a mighty barrier to a man.

"Go," cried he, "be not troubled for me, don't
retail so much wisdom, O busybody."

He answered, saying, "I am not thy enemy: it
would be a kindness if thou wouldst come
with me."

"I am sleepy," said he; "let me alone; go!"

That Muslim left the foolish man and returned
to his abode, muttering, "God help us!"

The man fell asleep, and the Bear kept driving
the flies away from his face, but they soon
came hurrying back again.

[1] As is declared in a Tradition of the Prophet.
[2] *i.e.* the *ignis fatuus* of carnality and vain desire.

The Bear went off in a rage and picked up a
very big stone from the mountain-side.

He fetched the stone, and seeing the flies again
settled on the face of his friend,

He took it up and struck at them to make them
go away.

The stone made powder of the sleeping man's
face and published to the whole world this
adage—

"Surely the love of a Fool is the love of a Bear:
his hate is love and his love is hate."

XVII

THE THIEF WHO SAID HE WAS A DRUMMER[1]

HEAR this parable—how a wicked Thief was cutting a hole at the bottom of a wall.

Someone who was ill and half awake heard the tapping of his pick.

And went on the roof and hung his head down and said to him, "What are you about, O father?

All is well, I hope. What are you doing here at midnight?

Who are you?" He said, "A drummer, O honourable sir."

"What are you about?" "I am beating the drum."

The sick man said, "Where is the noise of the drum, O artful one?"

He replied,"You will hear it to-morrow, namely, cries of 'Oh, alas!' and 'Oh, woe is me'! "

[1] Book III, v. 2799.

61

XVIII

THE GOLDSMITH WHO LOOKED
AHEAD[1]

A CERTAIN man came to a Goldsmith, saying,
"Give me the scales that I may weigh some
gold."

He replied, "Go, I have no sieve." "Give me
the scales," said the other, "and don't waste
time in jesting."

"There is no broom in the shop," said the
Goldsmith. "Enough! Enough!" he exclaimed; "leave these jokes.

Give me the scales I am asking for. Don't pretend to be deaf; don't talk at random."

He replied, "I heard what you said, I am not
deaf; you must not think I am nonsensical.

I heard your request, but you are a shaky old
man: your hand trembles and your body is
bowed;

And moreover your gold consists of tiny filings,
which will drop from your trembling hand.

Then you will say, 'Sir, fetch a broom, that I
may search in the dust for my gold';

[1] Book III, v. 1624.

And when you have gathered the sweepings,
you will tell me that you want the sieve.
I from the beginning discerned the end complete. Go from here to some other place, and
farewell!"

XIX

LUQMĀN AND HIS MASTER[1]

Luqmān was the favourite of his master, who
preferred him to his own sons,
Because Luqmān, though a slave, was master
of himself and free from sensual desire.
A certain King said to a holy man, "Ask a boon
that I may bestow it upon thee."
He answered, "O King, are not you ashamed
to say such a thing to me? Mount higher!
I have two slaves, and they are vile, and
yet those twain are rulers and lords over
you."
Said the King, "Who are those twain? Surely
this is an error." He replied, "The one is
anger and the other is lust."

Luqmān was always the first to partake of any
viands that were served to his master,
For the master would send them to him, and if
Luqmān left them untasted his master would
throw them away;
Or, if he did eat of them, it would be without

[1] Book II, v. 1462.

heart and without appetite: this is the sign
of an affinity without end.

One day he received the gift of a melon. "Go,"
said he, "call hither my dear Luqmān."

He gave him a slice: Luqmān ate it as though
it were sugar and honey,

And showed such pleasure that his master went
on giving him slice after slice, seventeen in all.

One slice remained. He said, "I will eat this
myself, to see what a sweet melon it is."

No sooner had he tasted it than its sourness
blistered his tongue and burnt his throat.

For a while he was almost beside himself;
then he cried, "O Luqmān, my soul and my
world,

How could you have the patience? What made
you endure so long? Or perhaps life is hateful
to you."

Luqmān said, "From thy bounteous hand I
have eaten so many sweets that I am bent
double with shame.

I was ashamed to refuse one bitter thing from
thy hand, O wise master.

Since all parts of me have grown from thy
bounty and are a prey to thy bait and snare—

If I complain of one bitter thing, may the dust
of a hundred roads cover every part of me!

This melon had reposed in thy sugar-bestow-
ing hand: how could it retain any bitterness?"

Through Love bitter things become sweet;
through Love pieces of copper become golden.
Through Love dregs become clear; through
Love pains become healing.
Through Love the dead is made living; through
Love the king is made a slave.

XX

THE LION AND THE BEASTS OF CHASE[1]

THE Beasts of Chase in a pleasant valley were
harassed by a Lion,

So they made a plan: they came to the Lion,
saying, "We will keep thee full-fed by a fixed
allowance.

Do not exceed thy allowance, else this pasture
will become bitter to us."

"Yes," said he, "if I find good faith on your
part, for I have suffered many a fraud at the
hands of Zayd and Bakr.[2]

I am done to death by the cunning of man, I
am stung by human snake and scorpion.

'The believer is not bitten twice': I have taken
this saying of the Prophet to my heart."

The Beasts said, "O sagacious one, let precaution
alone: it is of no avail against the divine Decree.

Precaution is but trouble and woe: put thy
trust in God, trust in God is better.

O fierce Lion, do not grapple with Destiny lest
Destiny pick a quarrel with thee."

[1] Book I, v. 900.
[2] Equivalent to "Tom, Dick, and Harry."

"Yes," he said; "but though trust in God is the true guide, yet we should use precaution according to the Prophet's rule.

The Prophet spoke plainly, saying, 'Trust in God, and bind the knee of thy camel.'

He hath also said, 'God loves the worker.' Let us trust in God, but not so as to neglect ways and means."

The Beasts answered him, saying, "There is no work better than trust in God: what indeed is dearer to Him than resignation?

Man contrives, and his contrivance is a snare to catch him: that which he thought would save his life sheds his blood.

He locks the door whilst his foe is in the house: the plot of Pharaoh was a tale of this kind.

We are the family of the Lord; like infants, we crave after milk.

God who gives rain from heaven is also able, in His mercy, to give us bread."

"Yes," said the Lion; "but the Lord hath set a ladder before our feet.

Step by step we must climb to the roof: to be a Necessitarian here is to indulge in foolish hopes.

You have feet: why do you pretend to be lame? You have hands: why do you hide your fingers?

When the master puts a spade in his slave's

68

hand, he need not speak in order to make his object known."

The Lion gave many proofs in this style, so that those Necessitarians became tired of answering him.

Fox and deer and hare and jackal abandoned their doctrine and ceased from disputation.

They made a covenant with the Lion, ensuring that he should incur no loss in the bargain,

And that he should receive his daily rations without trouble or any further demand.

Every day the one on whom the lot fell would run to the Lion as swiftly as a cheetah.

When the fatal cup came round to the Hare, "Why," cried the Hare, "how long shall we endure injustice?"

His companions said, "All this time we have sacrificed our lives in truth and loyalty.

Do not thou give us a bad name, O rebellious one! Quick! Quick! lest the Lion be aggrieved."

"O my friends," said he, "grant me a respite, that by my cunning ye may escape from this woe

And save your lives and leave security as a heritage to your children."

The Beasts replied, "O donkey, listen to us. Keep thyself within the measure of a hare!

Eh, what brag is this? Thy betters never thought of such a thing."

"My friends," said he, "God hath inspired me.
Weak as I am, I am wisely counselled.

God opens the door of knowledge to the bee,
so that it builds a house of honey.

God teaches the silkworm a craft beyond the
power of the elephant.

When Adam, the earth-born, gained knowledge of God, his knowledge illumined the
Seventh Heaven."

They said, "O nimble Hare, disclose what is
in thy mind. The Prophet hath said, 'Take
counsel with the trustworthy.' "

"Not every secret may be told," said he; "sometimes an even number turns out odd and an
odd one even.

If you breathe the hidden word on a mirror,
the mirror immediately becomes dim.

Hold your tongue concerning three things:
your departure, your money, and your religion."

The Hare tarried long, rehearsing to himself
the trick he was about to play.

At last he took the road and set forth to whisper
a few secrets in the Lion's ear.

The Lion, incensed and wrathful and frantic,
saw the Hare coming from afar,

Running undismayed and confidently, looking
angry and fierce and fell and sour;

For by appearing humble he thought suspicion
would be excited, while boldness would remove every cause of doubt.

As soon as he approached, the Lion roared,
"Ha, villain!

I who tear oxen limb from limb, I who bruise
the ears of the raging elephant—

What! shall a half-witted hare presume to spurn
my commands?"

"Mercy!" cried the Hare. "I have an excuse,
please thy Majesty."

"What excuse?" said he. "O the shortsighted-
ness of fools! Is this the time for them to
come into the presence of kings?

The fool's excuse is worse than his crime, 'tis
the poison that kills wisdom."

"Hark!" cried the Hare, "if I am not worthy of
thy clemency, I will lay my head before the
dragon of thy vengeance.

At breakfast-time I set out with another hare
which the Beasts of Chase had appointed,
for thy sake, to accompany me.

On the road a lion attacked thy humble slave,
attacked both the companions in travel hasten-
ing towards thee.

I said to him, 'We are the slaves of the King of
kings, two lowly fellow-servants of that exalted
Court.'

He said, 'The King of kings! Who is he? Be

71

ashamed! Do not make mention of every base
loon in my presence.

Both thee and thy King I will tear to pieces
if thou and thy friend turn back from my
portal.'

I said, 'Let me behold the face of my King
once more and acquaint him with the news
of thee.'

'Thou must leave thy comrade with me as a
pledge,' said he; 'otherwise thy life is forfeit
according to my law.'

We entreated him much: 'twas no use. He
seized my friend and left me to go my way
alone.

My friend was so big and plump and comely
that he would make three of me.

Henceforth the road is barred by that lion: the
cord of our covenant is broken.

Abandon hope of thy rations henceforward! I
am telling thee the bitter truth.

If thou want the rations, clear the road! Come
on, then, and drive away that insolent usur-
per!"

"Come on in God's name," cried the Lion.
"Show me where he is! Lead the way, if you
are speaking the truth,

That I may give him and a hundred like him the
punishment they deserve—or do the same
to you if you are lying."

The Hare set off, running ahead in the direction of a deep well which was to be a snare
for the Lion;

But as they drew nigh to it, the Hare shrunk
back. "That lion," said he, "lives here.

I am consumed with dread of his fury—unless
thou wilt take me beside thee,

That with thy support, O Mine of generosity,
I may open my eyes and look in."

The Lion took him to his side; they ran together
towards the well and looked in.

The Lion saw his own reflection: from the water
shone the image of a lion with a plump hare
beside him.

No sooner did he espy his adversary than he
left the Hare and sprang into the well.

He fell into the well which he had dug: his
iniquity recoiled on his own head.

The Lion saw himself in the well: he was so
enraged that he could not distinguish himself from his enemy.

O Reader, how many an evil that you see in
others is but your own nature reflected in
them!

In them appears all that you are—your hypocrisy,
iniquity, and insolence.

You do not see clearly the evil in yourself, else
you would hate yourself with all your soul.

Like the Lion who sprang at his image in the water, you are only hurting yourself, O simpleton!

When you reach the bottom of the well of your own nature, then you will know that the wickedness is in *you*.

XXI

THE SŪFĪ AND THE EMPTY WALLET[1]

ONE day a Sūfī espied a food-wallet hanging on
a nail; he began to whirl in the dance and
rend his garments,
Crying, "Lo, the food of the foodless! Lo, the
remedy for famine and pangs of hunger!"
When his smoke and tumult waxed great, every
one that was a Sūfī joined him.
They all shouted and shrieked and became
spiritually intoxicated and beside themselves.
An idle busybody said to the Sūfī, "What is
the matter? Only a food-wallet hung on a
nail, and it is empty of bread."
"Begone, begone!" he replied. "Thou art a
mere form without spirit. Go, seek existence,[2] for thou art no lover."

The lover's food is love of the bread, without
the existence of the bread. No true lover is
in thrall to existence.

[1] Book III, v. 3014.
[2] i.e. self-existence with all its egoistic wants and desires,
which is regarded by the lover of God as the greatest sin.

Lovers have naught to do with existence: lovers
have the interest without having the capital.
They have no wings, and yet they fly round
the world; they have no hands, and yet they
carry off the ball from the polo-field.

XXII

THE DIFFERENCE BETWEEN FEELING
AND THINKING[1]

SOMEONE slapped Zayd on the neck; Zayd
rushed at him with warlike purpose.
The assailant said, "I will ask thee a question.
First answer it, and then strike me.
I smote the nape of thy neck, and there was
the sound of a slap. At this point I have a
friendly question to ask thee.
Was the sound caused by my hand or by the
nape of thy neck, O pride of the noble?"
Zayd said, "On account of the pain I have no
time to reflect on this problem.
Do thou who art without pain reflect on it;
he that feels the pain cannot think of such
things."

---

[1] Book III, v. 1380. This is the second of two apologues
illustrating the attitude of emotional mysticism towards
scholastic theology. The first story concerns an elderly man
who was about to be married. He went to a barber and bade
him remove the white hairs in his beard, whereupon the
barber cut off the whole beard, laid it before his customer,
and said to him, "Pick them out yourself, I have important
business to attend to."

XXIII

THE GNAT AND THE WIND[1]

THE Gnat came from the garden and the grass
    and appealed to Solomon,
Saying, "O Solomon, thou dealest justice to
    the devils and the children of men and the
    genii.
Bird and fish are protected by thy justice:
    where is the wretch whom thy bounty has
    not sought out?
Give justice to us, for we are very miserable:
    we are deprived of the orchard and rose-
    garden.
The difficulties of every weakling are solved
    by thee: the Gnat in sooth is a proverb for
    weakness.
O thou who hast reached the limit in Power,
    while we have reached the limit in failure
    and aberration,
Do justice, relieve us of this sorrow, support
    us, O thou whose hand is the hand of
    God."
Then Solomon asked, "Against whom art thou
    demanding justice and equity, O suitor?

[1] Book III, v. 4624.

Who is the tyrant that in his insolence has done thee injury and scratched thy face?

Oh, wonderful! Where, in Our epoch, is the oppressor that is not in Our prison and chains?

When We were born, on that day Injustice died: who, then, has committed in Our epoch an act of injustice?

The Divine Will uttered in '*Be, and it was*' hath bestowed the Kingdom on Us, that the people may not cry in lament to Heaven;

That burning sighs may not soar upward; that the sky and the stars may not be shaken;

That the empyrean may not tremble at the orphan's wail; that no living soul may be marred by violence.

O oppressed one, do not look to Heaven, for thou hast a heavenly King in the temporal world."

"I appeal," said the Gnat, "against the fury of the Wind, for he hath opened the hands of oppression against us.

Through his oppression we are in sore straits: with closed lips we are drinking blood."[1]

Said Solomon, "O thou with the pretty voice, it behoves thee to hearken with all thy soul to the command of God,

[1] *i.e.* suffering torment.

God hath said to me, 'Beware, O Judge! Do not hear one litigant without the other.

Until both litigants come into the presence, the truth does not come to light before the judge.'

I dare not avert my face from the Divine command. Go, bring thy adversary before me."

"Thy words," said the Gnat, "are an argument conclusive and sound. My adversary is the Wind, and he is at thy behest."

The King shouted, "O Wind, the Gnat complains of thy injustice. Come!

Hark, come face to face with thy adversary and reply to him and rebut him."

When the Wind heard the summons, he came rapidly: the Gnat at once took to flight.

"O Gnat," cried Solomon, "where art thou going? Stop, that I may pass judgement upon you both."

The Gnat answered, "O King, his being is my death; verily, my day is made black by his smoke.

Since he has come, where shall I find peace? He wrings the vital breath out of my body."

Even such is the seeker at the Court of God: when God comes, the seeker is naughted.

Although union with God is life on life, yet at
    first that life consists in dying to self.
The shadows that seek the Light are naughted
    when His Light appears.
How should reason remain when He bids it go?
    Everything is perishing except His Face.[1]

---

[1] *Qur'ān*, xxviii, 88.

XXIV

THE PRINCE WHO WAS BEATEN AT CHESS BY THE COURT-JESTER[1]

THE Prince of Tirmidh was playing chess with
Dalqak. When Dalqak mated him, his anger
burst.

On hearing the word "Checkmate!" the haughty
monarch threw the chessmen, one by one, at
Dalqak's head.

"Here, take your 'checkmate,'" he cried, "you
scoundrel!" Dalqak controlled himself and
only said, "Mercy!"

Then the Prince commanded him to play again.

He obeyed, trembling like a naked man in bitter
cold.

The Prince lost the second game too, but when
the moment arrived to say 'Checkmate!'

Dalqak jumped up, ran into a corner, and
hastily flung six rugs over himself.

There he lay hidden beneath six rugs and several
cushions in order to escape the Prince's blows.

"Hey!" said the Prince, "what are you doing?
What is this?" "Checkmate! Checkmate! Checkmate!" he replied, "O noble Prince."

[1] Book V, v. 3507.

XXV

THE INFANT MOHAMMED AND THE IDOLS[1]

I WILL tell you the story of Halīma's mystic experience,[2] that her tale may clear away your trouble.

When she parted Mustafā[3] from her milk, she took him up on the palm of her hand as though he were sweet basil and roses.

Fearing for the safety of her precious charge, she went towards the Ka'ba and entered the Hatīm.[4]

From the air she heard a voice saying, "O Hatīm, an exceedingly mighty Sun hath shone upon thee.

O Hatīm, to-day there marches into thee with pomp a glorious King, whose harbinger is Fortune.

O Hatīm, to-day thou wilt surely become anew the abode of exalted spirits.

[1] Book IV, *v.* 915.
[2] Halīma, a Bedouin woman, is said to have been Mohammed's nurse and foster-mother.
[3] Mohammed.
[4] The name Hatīm is properly given to a semi-circular wall adjoining the north and west corners of the Ka'ba. Here it denotes the space between the wall and the Ka'ba.

83

The spirits of the holy will come to thee from
every quarter in troops and multitudes,
drunken with desire."

Halīma was bewildered by that voice, for neither
in front nor behind was anyone to be seen.

She laid Mustafā on the earth, that she might
search after the sweet sound;

Then she cast her eyes to and fro, saying,
"Where is that kingly crier of mysteries?"

Seeing no one, she became distraught and
despairing: her body trembled like a willow-
bough.

She returned towards that righteous Child, but
could not see Mustafā where she had left
him.

Amazement fell upon her heart: a great dark-
ness of grief encompassed her.

She ran to the dwellings hard by, crying, "Alas,
who has carried off my single Pearl?"

The Meccans said, "We have no knowledge:
we knew not that a child was there."

She shed so many tears and made such a lamentation that all began to weep for her.

Beating her breast, she sobbed so mightily that
the stars were made to sob by her sobbing.

An old man with a staff approached her, saying,
"Why, what hath befallen thee, O Halīma?"

She replied, "I am Mohammed's trusted foster-

mother: I was taking him back to his grand-
sire.

When I arrived in the Hatīm, I heard voices
from the air and laid the Child down,

To see whence the sounds came that were so
melodious and beautiful.

I saw no sign of anyone about, yet the voices
never ceased for a moment.

I was lost in bewilderment. On coming to myself, I could not see the Child. Oh, the sorrow
of my heart!"

"Daughter," said the old man, "do not grieve.
I will show unto thee a Queen,

Who, if she wish, will tell thee what has happened to the Child: she knows where he went
and where he is now."

He brought her to 'Uzzā,[1] saying, "This Idol
is greatly prized for information concerning
the Unseen.

Through her we have found thousands who
were lost, when we betook ourselves to her
in devotion."

Then he bowed low before her and said, "O
Sovereign of the Arabs, O Sea of munificence,

Thou hast done many favours to us, O 'Uzzā,
so that we have been delivered from snares.

[1] One of three goddesses whom the pre-Islamic Arabs
worshipped as daughters of Allah.

In hope of thee this Halīma of the tribe Sa'd
hath come under the shadow of thy bounty,

For an infant child of hers is lost: the name of
the child is Mohammed."

When he pronounced the name "Mohammed"
all the Idols at once fell headlong and prostrate,

Saying, "Begone, old man! Why dost thou
inquire after this Mohammed by whom we
are deposed?

By him we are overthrown and reduced to a
heap of stones: by him we are made con-
temptible and worthless.

Avaunt, old man! Do not kindle mischief.
Hark, do not burn us in the flame of Mohammed's jealousy.

Avaunt, old man, for God's sake, lest thou too
be burnt in the fire of Fore-ordainment.

What squeezing of the dragon's tail is this?
Hast thou any inkling what the news of Mohammed's advent is?

At these tidings the heart of sea and mine will
surge; at these tidings the Seven Heavens
will tremble."

The old man's staff dropped from his hand;
his teeth chattered; like a naked man in
winter, he shuddered and cried, "Woe is me."

When Halīma saw him in such a state of terror,
self-control deserted her.

"Once before," she cried, "they of the Invisible
carried off my Child—they of the Invisible,
the green-winged ones of Heaven.
Of whom shall I complain? Whom shall I tell?
I am crazy and in a hundred minds.
His jealousy hath closed my lips, so that I cannot declare the mystery: I can only say, 'My
Child is lost.'
If I should say aught else now, the people would
bind me with chains as though I were mad."
The old man said to her, "O Halīma, rejoice;
bow down in thanksgiving, and do not rend
thy face.
Do not grieve: he will not be lost to thee; nay,
but the whole world will be lost in him.
Always, before and behind, he hath myriads of
zealous guardians watching over him.
Didst not thou see how the Idols, with all their
magic arts, fell headlong at the name of thy
Child?
This is a marvellous epoch on the earth: I am
grown old, but never have I witnessed aught
like this."

XXVI

THE SŪFĪS WHO SOLD THE TRAVELLER'S ASS[1]

A Sūfī, after journeying, arrived at a monastery
　　for dervishes; he took his mount and led it
　　to the stable.

With his own hand he gave it a little water and
　　some fodder: he was not such a Sūfī as the
　　one we told of before.[2]

He took precautions against neglect and foolish-
　　ness, but when the Divine destiny comes to
　　pass, of what avail is precaution?

The Sūfīs were poor and destitute: poverty
　　almost entails an infidelity that brings the
　　soul to perdition.

O thou rich man who art full-fed, beware of
　　mocking at the unrighteousness of the suffer-
　　ing poor.

On account of their destitution that Sūfī flock
　　adopted the expedient of selling the Ass,

Saying, "In case of necessity a carcase is law-
　　ful food: many a vicious act is made virtuous
　　by necessity."

[1] Book II, v. 514.
[2] See Story IV.

Having sold the little Ass, they fetched dainty
   viands and lit candles.

Jubilation arose in the monastery. "To-night,"
   they cried, "there shall be dainties and music
   and dancing and voracity.

No more of this carrying the beggar's wallet, no
   more of this abstinence and three-days' fasting!"

The Traveller, tired by the long journey, rejoiced to see the favour with which they
   regarded him.

One by one they caressed him and played the
   game of bestowing pleasant attentions on him.

When he saw this, he said, "If I don't make
   merry to-night, when shall I have such good
   reasons for it again?"

They consumed the viands and began the *samā* ;[1]
   the monastery was filled with smoke and dust
   up to the roof—

The smoke of the kitchen, the dust raised by
   the dancing feet, the tumult of soul aroused
   by longing and ecstasy.

Now, waving their hands, they would beat the
   floor with their feet; now, bowing low, they
   would sweep the dais with their foreheads.

Only after long waiting does the Sūfī gain his
   desire from Fortune; hence the Sūfī is a
   great eater;

Except, to be sure, the Sūfī who has eaten his

[1] The musical dance of Muslim dervishes.

fill of the Light of God: he is free from the shame of beggary;

But of these there are only a few amongst thousands; the rest live under the protection of his (the perfect Sūfī's) spiritual empire.

When the *samā'* had run its course from beginning to end, the minstrel struck up a deep-sounding strain.

He sang "The Ass is gone, the Ass is gone," and made the whole company sharers in the ditty.

Till daybreak they were dancing rapturously, clapping their hands and singing "The Ass is gone, the Ass is gone, my son!"

By way of imitation, that Sūfī began to sing in tones of impassioned feeling the same phrase, "The Ass is gone."

When the pleasure and excitement and music and dancing were over, day dawned and they all said farewell.

The monastery was deserted and the Sūfī remained alone: he set about shaking the dust from his baggage.

He brought out the baggage from his cell to pack it on the Ass, for he desired companions on his journey.

He made haste to join his fellow-travellers, but when he went into the stable he did not find the Ass.

"The servant," he said to himself, "has taken
it to water, because it drank little water last
night."

When the servant came the Sūfī asked, "Where
is the Ass?" "Look at your beard,"[1] he replied; and this started a quarrel.

The Sūfī said, "I entrusted the Ass to you. I
put you in charge of the Ass.

Discuss the matter reasonably, don't argue, but
deliver back to me what I delivered to you;

And if you obstinately refuse, then look here,
let us go for judgement to the Cadi!"

The servant said, "I was overpowered: the Sūfīs
rushed on me, and I was in fear of my life.

Do you throw a liver with the parts next it
amongst cats and then seek the traces of it?

One cake of bread amongst a hundred hungry
people, one starved cat before a hundred dogs?"

"I grant," said the Sūfī, "that they took the
Ass from you by violence, aiming at the life
of wretched me;

But you never came and said, 'They are taking
away your Ass, O dervish,'

So that I might have bought it back from the
purchaser, or else they might have divided
the money[2] amongst themselves.

[1] *i.e.* "don't ask childish questions."
[2] The money which the Sūfī would have paid as a ransom
for his Ass.

There were a hundred ways of mending the
matter when they were present, but now each
one is gone to a different clime.

Why didn't you come and say, 'O stranger, a
terrible outrage has been committed'? "

"By God!" said he, "I came several times to
inform you of these doings,

But you went on singing 'The Ass is gone, O
son' with more gusto than all the others;

So I was always going away, saying to myself,
'He is aware of it, he is satisfied with what
God has decreed, he is a gnostic.' "

The Sūfī replied, "They all sang it so gleefully,
and I too felt delight in singing it.

Blind imitation of them has brought me to ruin:
a thousand curses on that imitation!"

XXVII

THE FOUR BEGGARS WHO WISHED TO BUY GRAPES[1]

A CERTAIN man gave a dirhem to four Beggars. One of them, a Persian, said, "I will spend it on *angūr*."

The second, who was an Arab, cried, "Nay, I want *'inab*, not *angūr*, you rascal!"

The third was a Turk: he said, "The money is mine: I don't want *'inab*, I want *uzum*."

The fourth, being a Greek, said, "Stop this talk: I want *istāfīl*."[2]

They began to fight because they were unaware of the meaning of the words.

In their folly they smote each other with their fists: they were full of ignorance and empty of knowledge.

This difference cannot be removed till a spiritual Solomon, skilled in tongues,[3] shall intervene.

O ye wrangling birds, hearken, like the falcon, to the falcon-drum of the King!

[1] Book II, *v*. 3681.

[2] σταφυλή.

[3] According to the *Qur'ān*, Solomon was acquainted with the speech of birds and animals.

93

Come now, from every quarter set out with joy, flying away from diversity towards Oneness.

Wheresoever ye be, turn your faces towards it:[1] this is the thing He hath not forbidden unto you at any time.

[1] *Qur'ān*, II, 145.

XXVIII

MOSES AND THE SHEPHERD[1]

MOSES saw a shepherd on the way, who was
    saying, "O God who choosest as Thou wilt,
Where art Thou, that I may become Thy ser-
    vant and sew Thy shoes and comb Thy head?
That I may wash Thy clothes and kill Thy lice
    and bring milk to Thee, O worshipful One;
That I may kiss Thy little hand and rub Thy little
    feet and sweep Thy little room at bedtime."
On hearing these foolish words, Moses said,
    "Man, to whom are you speaking!"
He answered, "To Him who created us and
    brought this earth and heaven to sight."
"Hark!" said Moses, "you are a very wicked
    man: indeed you are no true believer, you
    have become an infidel.
What babble is this? What blasphemy and
    raving? Stuff some cotton into your mouth!
The stench of your blasphemy hath made the
    whole world stink: your blasphemy hath
    torn the mantle of Religion to rags.
Shoes and socks are fitting for you, but how
    are such things right for the Lord of glory?

[1] Book II, *v.* 1720.

95

Truly, the friendship of a fool is enmity:
the high God is not in want of suchlike
service."

The shepherd said, "O Moses, thou hast closed
my mouth and thou hast burned my soul
with contrition."

He rent his garment, heaved a sigh, turned in
haste towards the desert and went his way.

A Revelation came to Moses from God—"Thou
hast parted My servant from Me.

Wert thou sent as a prophet to unite, or wert
thou sent to sever?

I have bestowed on everyone a particular mode
of worship, I have given everyone a peculiar
form of expression.

In regard to him these words are praiseworthy,
in regard to thee blameworthy: honey for
him, poison for thee.

The idiom of Hindustān is excellent in the
Hindūs; the idiom of Sind is excellent in the
people of Sind.

I look not at tongue and speech, I look at the
spirit and the inward feeling.

I gaze into the heart to see whether it be lowly,
though the words uttered be not lowly.

Enough of phrases and conceptions and meta-
phors! I want burning, burning: become
familiar with that burning!

Light up a fire of love in thy soul, burn all
thought and expression away!
O Moses, they that know the conventions are
of one sort, they whose souls and spirits burn
are of another sort."

The Religion of Love is apart from all religions.
The lovers of God have no religion but God
alone.

XXIX

THE CAT AND THE MEAT[1]

THERE was a man, a householder, who had a
    very sneering, sluttish, and rapacious wife.

She would devour everything he brought
    home, and the poor man was reduced to
    silence.

One day, having a guest, he brought home some
    meat which had cost him infinite toil and
    hardship.

His wife ate it up; she consumed all the *kabāb*[2]
    and wine, and when her husband came in she
    put him off with lies.

"Where is the meat?" he asked. "Our guest
    has arrived: one must set nice food before a
    guest."

"The cat has eaten it," said she; "go and buy
    some more if possible."

He called his servant. "Fetch the scales, Aybak:
    I will weigh the cat."

He found that the cat weighed half a maund.[3]

    "O deceitful woman," he cried,

---

[1] Book V, *v.* 3409.

[2] Roast meat.

[3] The *man* (maund) is about two pounds avoirdupois.

"The meat was half a maund and six drachms over, and the cat is just half a maund, my lady!

If this is the cat, then where is the meat? or if this is the meat, where is the cat?"

XXX

HOW BĀYAZĪD PERFORMED THE
PILGRIMAGE[1]

ON his way to the Ka'ba, Bāyazīd sought earn-
estly to meet the Khizr of the age.[2]

He espied an old man whose body was curved
like the new moon; in him was the majesty
and lofty speech of saints;

His eyes sightless, his heart radiant as the sun;
like an elephant dreaming of Hindustān,

Beholding with closed eyes a hundred delights;
when his eyes open, he sees naught thereof.
How wonderful!

Many a wonder is made manifest in sleep: in
sleep the heart becomes a window.

He that is awake and dreams fair dreams is the
knower of God: smear your eyes with his
dust!

Bāyazīd sat down before him and asked about

[1] Book II, v. 2231. Bāyazīd of Bistām was a famous
Persian Sūfī of the ninth century.

[2] i.e. the supreme head of the hierarchy of saints. Khizr,
sometimes identified with Elijah, is a mysterious personage
who gained immortality by drinking of the Water of Life.
The Sūfīs believe that he meets them in their wanderings,
or appears in their visions, and imparts to them all sorts of
esoteric lore.

his condition: he found him to be a dervish and also a family man.

"O Bāyazīd," said he, "whither art thou faring? To what place wouldst thou take the baggage of travel in a strange land?"

Bāyazīd answered, "I start for the Ka'ba at daybreak." "Eh," cried the other, "what hast thou as provision for the road?"

"Two hundred silver dirhems," said he. "Here they are, tied in the corner of my cloak."

He said, "Make a circuit seven times round me, and reckon this to be better than the circumambulation of the Ka'ba;

And lay the dirhems before me, O generous man. Know that thou hast made the Greater Pilgrimage[1] and won to thy desire,

And thou hast performed the Lesser Pilgrimage[2] too and gained the life everlasting, and thou hast run up the Hill of Purity[3] and been purged.

By the truth of the Truth which thy soul hath seen, I swear that He hath chosen me above His House.

Albeit the Ka'ba is the House of His worship, my form in which I was created is the House of His inmost mystery.

[1] *Hajj.*
[2] *'Umra.*
[3] The Hill *Safā*, which the pilgrims ascend after having performed the ceremony of circumambulation (*tawāf*).

Never since God made the Ka'ba hath He
entered it, and none but the Living God
hath ever entered into this House of mine.

When thou hast seen me thou hast seen God:
thou hast circled round the true Ka'ba.

To serve me is to obey and glorify God. Beware! Deem not that God is separate from
me.

Open thine eyes well and look on me, that thou
mayst behold the Light of God in man."

Bāyazīd gave heed to these mystic sayings and
put them as a golden ring in his ear.

XXXI

THE ARAB OF THE DESERT AND HIS DOG[1]

THE dog was dying, the Arab was shedding tears and crying, "Woe is me!"

A passing beggar asked him the cause of his tears, and for whom he was making such a lament.

He replied, "I owned a dog of excellent disposition; look, he is dying on the road.

He hunted for me by day and kept watch at night; he was a sharp-eyed hunter and a driver away of thieves."

"What is the matter with him? Has he been wounded?" "No; the pangs of hunger have brought him to the last gasp."

"Show patience in this trouble and affliction: the grace of God bestows a recompense on those who suffer patiently."

Afterwards the beggar said to him, "O noble chief, what is inside this well-filled wallet in your hand?"

"Bread," said he, "and the remnants of last night's meal: I am taking them with me to nourish my body."

[1] Book V, *v.* 477.

"Why don't you give them to the dog?" "I
have not love and charity to that extent.
One cannot get bread on the road without spend-
ing money, but tears cost nothing."
"Dust on thy head," cried the beggar, "thou
water-skin full of wind! To thee a crust of
bread is more precious than tears."

XXXII

THE TEACHER WHO IMAGINED HE WAS ILL[1]

THE boys in a certain school, who suffered at the
hands of their master from weariness and toil,
Consulted how they might stop his work and
compel him to let them go.
One, the cleverest of them all, proposed that
he should say, "Master, why are you so pale?
I hope you are well. You have lost your colour:
is it the effect of bad air or of fever?"
He continued, "On hearing this he will begin
to fancy that he is ill. Do you too, brother,
help me in like manner.
When you come in through the school door
say to him, 'Master, is your health good?'
Then that fancy of his will increase a little, for
fancy can drive a sensible man mad.
After us, let the third boy and the fourth and
fifth show the same sympathy and concern,
So that, when thirty boys in succession tell this
story, it may settle down in his mind."
"Bravo!" cried the boys; "may your fortune rest
on God's favour, O sagacious one!"

[1] Book III, v. 1522.

They agreed, in firm covenant, that no fellow
should alter the words;
And then, lest any tell-tale should reveal the
plot, he administered an oath to them all.
The counsel of that boy prevailed over his companions; his intellect was the leader of the
flock.
There is the same difference in human minds
as in the outward forms of those who are
beloved.[1]
From this point of view Mohammed said that a
man's excellence lies hidden in his tongue.[2]

Next day, thinking of nothing else, the boys
came from their homes to the "shop,"
And stood outside, waiting for that resolute
fellow to go in first,
Because he was the source of the plan: the head
is always an Imām to the foot.
He went in and said to the master, "Salaam! I
hope you are well: you look pale."
The master said, "I have no ailment. Go and sit
down and don't talk nonsense, hey!"
He denied it, but the dust of vain imagination
struck a little upon his mind.

[1] The poet's doctrine of the innate difference in human
intellects is opposed to that of the Mu'tazilites, who held
that men are originally equal in this respect and that all
diversities arise from learning and experience.
[2] *i.e.* until he speaks, no one can judge of his intelligence.

Another boy came in and said the like, which
    strengthened that imagination a little more;
And so on and so on, till at last he was exceed-
    ingly alarmed as to his state of health.
The master became unnerved; he sprang up
    and slowly made his way home,
Angry with his wife and saying, "Her love is
    weak: I am so ill, and she never asked or
    inquired;
She did not even inform me about my colour:
    she is ashamed of me and wishes to be free."
He came home and fiercely opened the door,
    the boys following at his heels.
His wife said, "Is it well with thee? How hast
    thou come so soon? May no evil happen to
    thy goodly person!"
He said, "Are you blind? Look at my colour
    and appearance; even strangers are lament-
    ing my affliction,
While you, within my house, from hatred and
    hypocrisy, do not see what anguish I am
    suffering."
"O Sir," said his wife, "there is nothing wrong
    with thee: 'tis only thy vain fancy and opinion."
He replied, "Will you still be wrangling, O
    harlot? Don't you see the change in my looks
    and how I tremble?
If you are blind and deaf, what fault of mine is
    it? I am in pain and grief and woe."

She said, "Sir, I will bring the mirror in order that thou mayst know I am innocent."

"Begone," said he; "a plague on you and your mirror! You are always engaged in hatred and malice and sin.

Lay my bed at once, that I may lie down, for my head is sore."

The wife lingered; he bawled at her, "Be quick, odious creature! This is just like you!"

The old woman brought the bed-clothes and spread them. She said to herself, "I can do no more, though my heart is burning.

If I speak, he will suspect me; and if I say nothing, the affair will become serious.

If I tell him he is not ill, he will imagine that I have an evil design and am making arrangements to be alone.

'She is getting me out of the house,' he will say; 'she is plotting some wickedness.' "

As soon as the bed was made the master threw himself down, sighing and moaning continually,

While the boys sat round, reciting their lesson with a hundred sorrows in secret,

Thinking, "We have done all this, and still we are detained: it was a badly built plan and we are bad builders."

The clever boy said, "O good fellows, recite the lesson and make your voices loud."

When they raised their voices he said, "Boys, the noise we are making will do the master harm.

His headache will increase: is it worth his while to suffer such pain for the sake of a few pence?"

The master said, "He is right. Go away! My headache is worse. Get out!"

They bowed and said, "O honoured Sir, may illness and danger be far from you!"

Then they bounded off to their homes, like birds in quest of grain.

Their mothers were angry with them and said, "A school-day and you at play!"

Each boy offered excuses, saying, "Stop, mother! This sin does not proceed from us and is not caused by our fault.

By the destiny of Heaven our master has become ill and sick and afflicted."

The mothers said, "It is a trick and a lie: ye invent a hundred lies in your greed for amusement.

To-morrow we will visit the master, that we may see what is at the bottom of this trick of yours."

"Go in God's name," said the boys, "and find out whether we are lying or telling the truth."

Next morning the mothers came and found the
    master in bed, like one who is gravely ill,

Perspiring under a great many coverlets, his
    head bandaged and his face enveloped in the
    quilt.

He was moaning softly. They all began to cry,
    "*Lā hawl.*"[1]

They said, "Master, may all be well! This
    headache—by thy soul, we were not aware of
    it."

"Neither was I," said he, "till these rascals
    called my attention to it.

I was teaching and too busy to take notice,
    though such a grave malady lurked within
    me."

[1] See p. 17, note 2.

XXXIII

THE UNSEEN ELEPHANT[1]

THE Elephant was in a dark house: some Hindūs
  had brought it for exhibition.
As seeing it with the eye was impossible, every-
  one felt it in the dark with the palm of his
  hand.
The hand of one fell on its trunk: he said, "This
  creature is like a water-pipe."
Another touched its ear: to him it appeared
  like a fan.
Another handled its leg: he said, "I found the
  Elephant's shape to be like a pillar."
Another laid his hand on its back: he said,
  "Truly this Elephant resembles a throne."
Had there been a candle in each one's hand, the
  difference would have gone out of their words.

---

[1] Book III, *v.* 1259. Religions are many, but God is One.
The intellect, groping in the dark, cannot form any true
conception of His nature. Only the clairvoyant eye of the
mystic sees Him as he really is.

XXXIV

PHARAOH AND HIS MAGICIANS[1]

WHEN Moses had returned home, Pharaoh
called his advisers and counsellors to his
presence.

They deemed it right that the King and Ruler
of Egypt should assemble the magicians from
all parts of Egypt.

Thereupon he sent many men in every direction
to collect the sorcerers.

In whatsoever region there was a renowned
magician, he sent flying towards him ten
active couriers.

There were two youths, famous magicians:
their magic penetrated into the heart of the
moon.

They milked the moon publicly and openly; in
their journeys they went mounted on a wine-
jar.

They caused the moonshine to seem like a piece
of linen; they measured and sold it speedily

And took the silver away: the purchaser, on
becoming aware of the fraud, would smite his
hand upon his cheeks in grief.

[1] Book III, *v.* 1157.

They invented a hundred thousand such tricks
of sorcery and did not follow behind, like
the rhyme-letter.[1]

When the King's message reached them, to
this effect: "The King desires your aid,

Because two dervishes[2] have come and marched
against the King and his palace.

They have naught with them except a rod,
which becomes a dragon at his command.

The King and the whole army are helpless: all
have been brought to lamentation by these
twain.

A remedy must be sought in magic, that maybe
ye will save their lives from these enchan-
ters"—

When the King's courier gave the message to
the two young magicians, a great fear and
love descended on the hearts of them both.

The vein of spiritual affinity began to throb,[3]
and in amazement they laid their heads upon
their knees.

Inasmuch as the knee is the Sūfī's school,[4] the
two knees are sorcerers for solving a difficulty.

[1] *i.e.* they did not imitate others.
[2] Moses and Aaron.
[3] Because God had predestined them to have faith in
Moses and become his followers.
[4] Referring to the attitude of Sūfīs when engaged in holy
meditation.

How those two magicians summoned their father from the grave and questioned their father's spirit concerning the real nature of Moses, on whom be peace.

Afterwards they said, "Come, O mother, where is our father's grave? Do thou show us the way."

She led them to his grave: there they kept a three-days' fast for the sake of the King.

Then they said, "O father, the King in consternation hath sent us a message

That two men have brought him to sore straits and destroyed his prestige with the army.

There is not with them any weapons or soldiers; nothing but a rod, and in the rod is a calamity and bane.

Thou art gone into the world of the righteous, though to outward seeming thou liest in a tomb.

If that be magic, inform us; and if it be divine, O spirit of our father,

In that case too inform us, so that we may bow down before them and bring ourselves in touch with an elixir.[1]

We are despairing, and a hope has come; we are banished, and Mercy has drawn us back."

[1] The prophets and saints are often compared to the Philosophers' Stone which transmutes base metal into pure gold.

How the dead Magician answered his sons.

He cried, "O my dearest sons, it rests with God
to declare this matter plainly.

It is not permitted to me to speak openly and
freely, though the mystery is not far from
mine eye;

But I will show unto you a sign, that this hidden
thing may be made manifest to you.

O light of mine eyes, when ye go thither become acquainted with the place where he
sleeps,

And at the time when that Sage is asleep make
for the rod, abandon fear.

If thou art able to steal it, he is a magician: the
means of dealing with a magician are present
with thee;

But if thou canst not steal it, beware, beware!
That man is of God, he is the messenger of
the Almighty and is divinely guided.

Let Pharaoh occupy the world from east to
west, he will fall headlong. God and then
war![1]

I give thee this true sign, O soul of thy father,
inscribe it in thy heart: God best knoweth
the truth.

O soul of thy father, when a magician sleeps,
there is none to direct his magic and craft.

---

[1] *i.e.* the idea of opposing God is absurd.

When the shepherd has gone to sleep, the wolf
  becomes unafraid; when he falls asleep, his
  work is done;
But what hope or way hath the wolf to reach
  the animal whose shepherd is God?
O soul of thy father, this is the decisive sign:
  even if a prophet die, God exalteth him."[1]

*Comparison of the sublime Qur'ān to the rod of
Moses, and the death of Mohammed, on whom
be peace, to the sleep of Moses, and those who
would alter the Qur'ān to the two young Magicians who attempted to carry off the rod of Moses
when they found him asleep.*

The lovingkindness of God made a promise to
  Mohammed, saying, "If thou shalt die, yet
  this Lesson[2] shall not die.
I will exalt thy Book and Miracle, I will defend
  the *Qur'ān* from those who would make it
  more or less.
I will exalt thee in both worlds, I will drive
  away the scoffers from thy Tidings.
None shall be able to add or omit therein. Do
  not thou seek a guardian better than Me.

[1] The conclusion of the Story may be summarised in a
few words. When the two Magicians approach Moses, the
Rod turns into a Dragon. They flee in panic, are stricken
with fever, and at the point of death entreat Moses to pardon
their presumption, acknowledging him to be the prophet of
God.

[2] The *Qur'ān*.

Day by day I will increase thy splendour; I
will strike thy name on gold and silver.

For thy sake I will prepare pulpit and prayer-
niche: in My love for thee thy vengeance
hath become My vengeance.

Thy followers, from fear, utter thy name
covertly and hide when they perform their
prayers;

From terror and dread of the accursed infidels
thy Religion is hidden underground;

But I will fill the world from end to end with
minarets; I will blind the eyes of the recalci-
trant.

Thy servants will occupy cities and seize power:
thy Religion will extend from the Fish to the
Moon.[1]

I will keep it living until the Resurrection: be
not thou afraid of the annulment of thy
Religion, O Mustafā!

O My Prophet, thou art not a sorcerer: thou art
truthful, thou wearest the mantle of Moses.

To thee the *Qur'ān* is even as the rod of Moses:
it swallows up infidelities like a dragon.

If thou sleepest beneath a sod, yet deem as his
rod My Word which thou hast spoken.

Assailants have no power over his rod. Sleep,
then, O King, a blessed sleep!

[1] The Earth was supposed by Muslim cosmogonists to
rest on the back of a Fish floating in a great Ocean.

Whilst thy body is asleep in the tomb, thy Light
in Heaven[1] hath strung a bow for thy war
against the infidels.

The philosopher and that which his mouth
doeth—the bow of thy Light is piercing them
with arrows."

Thus He did, and even more than He said.
The Prophet slept, but his fortune and prosperity slumbered not.

---

[1] The pre-existent form of Mohammed, which is the first
thing that God created, was conceived as a celestial Light:
this Light (*Nūr Muhammadī*) became incarnate in Adam
and in the whole series of prophets after him from generation
to generation until its final appearance in the historical
Mohammed himself. According to the Shī'ites, however, it
passed from Mohammed to 'Alī and the Imāms of his
House, while the Sūfī saints also claim to be its torch-
bearers.

XXXV

THE MOST BEAUTIFUL CITY[1]

A LOVED one said to her lover, "O youth, thou
    hast seen many cities abroad.
Which of them, then, is the fairest?" He re-
    plied, "The city where my sweetheart dwells."
Wherever the carpet is spread for our King 'tis
    a spacious plain though it be narrow as the
    eye of a needle.
Wherever there is a Joseph beautiful as the
    moon, 'tis Paradise, even if it be the bottom
    of a well.

[1] Book III, *v.* 3808.

119

XXXVI

THE PATIENCE OF LUQMĀN[1]

LUQMĀN went to David, the pure of heart, and
　　observed that he was making rings of iron,
And that the exalted King was casting the rings
　　into each other.[2]
He had not seen the armourer's handicraft be-
　　fore: he was astonished, and his curiosity
　　increased—
"What can this be? I will ask him what he is
　　making with the interwoven rings."
Again he said to himself, "Patience is better:
　　patience is the quickest guide to the object
　　of one's search."
When you ask no questions, the sooner will the
　　secret be disclosed to you: the bird, patience,
　　flies faster than all others;
And if you ask, the more slowly will your object
　　be gained: what is easy will be made difficult
　　by your impatience.
When Luqmān kept silence, straightway the
　　ring-making was finished by David's crafts-
　　manship.

[1] Book III, v. 1842.
[2] God taught David the art of making coats of mail
(*Qur'ān*, xxi, 80).

Then he fashioned a coat of mail and put it on in the presence of the noble and patient Luqmān.

"This," he said, "is an excellent garment, O young man, for warding off blows on the battlefield."

Luqmān said, "Patience too is of good effect, for it is the protection and defence against pain everywhere."

XXXVII

HOW JESUS FLED FROM THE FOOLS[1]

JESUS, son of Mary, was fleeing to a mountain:
you would say that a lion wished to shed his
blood.

A certain man ran after him and said, "Is it
well? There is none pursuing thee: why art
thou fleeing like a bird?"

But Jesus still ran on so quickly that on account
of his haste he did not answer him.

The man went in pursuit of Jesus for the dis-
tance of one or two fields; then he invoked
Jesus with the utmost earnestness,

Saying, "For God's sake, stop one moment! I
have a difficulty concerning thy flight.

From whom art thou fleeing, O noble one? No
lion is chasing thee, no enemy, and there is
no fear or danger."

He said, "I am fleeing from the fool. Begone! I am saving myself. Do not hinder
me!"

"Why," said he, "art not thou the Messiah by
whom the blind and deaf are restored to
sight and hearing?"

[1] Book III, *v.* 2570.

He said, "Yea." Said the other, "Art not thou the King in whom the spells of the Unseen World have their abode,

So that, when thou chantest them over a dead man, he springs up like a lion that has caught his prey?"

He said, "Yea, I am he." Said the other, "Dost not thou make living birds out of clay,[1] O beauteous one?"

He said, "Yea." Said the other, "Then, O pure Spirit, thou doest whatsoever thou wilt: of whom hast thou fear?

With such miraculous evidence, who in the world would not be a slave devoted to thee?"

Jesus said, "By the holy Essence of God, the Maker of the body and the Creator of the soul in eternity;

By the sanctity of the pure Essence and Attributes of Him for whose sake the collar of Heaven is rent,

I swear that the spells and the Most Great Name which I pronounced over the deaf and blind were good in their effects.

I pronounced them over the stony mountain: it was cloven and tore upon itself its mantle down to the navel.

I pronounced them over the corpse: it came to

[1] *Qur'ān*, III, 43.

123

life. I pronounced them over nonentity: it became entity.

I pronounced them lovingly over the heart of the fool hundreds of thousands of times, and 'twas no cure for his folly."

XXXVIII

THE MAN WHO THOUGHT HE HAD
PRAYED TO GOD IN VAIN[1]

ONE night a certain man was crying "Allah!"
till his lips grew sweet with praise of Him.

The Devil said, "Prithee, O garrulous one,
where is the response 'Here am I' to all this
'Allah'?

Not a single response is coming from the
Throne: how long will you cry 'Allah' with
grim face?"

He became broken-hearted and lay down to
sleep: in a dream he saw Khadir[2] amidst the
verdure,

Who said, "Hark, you have held back from
praising God: why do you repent of having
called unto Him?"

He replied, "No 'Here am I' is coming to me
in response, hence I fear that I am turned
away from the Door."

Said Khadir, "Nay; God saith, 'That 'Allah'
of thine is My 'Here am I,' and that suppli-

---

[1] Book III, *v.* 189.
[2] For Khadir or Khizr, see p. 100, note 2.

125

cation and grief and ardour of thine is My messenger to thee.

Thy fear and love are the noose to catch My favour: beneath every 'O Lord' of thine is many a 'Here am I' from Me.'"

XXXIX

THE HOUSE BUILT ON HYPOTHESES[1]

A HOMELESS man was hastily seeking a house.
   One of his friends took him to a house in
   ruins
And remarked, "If it had a roof, it would do
   for you to live in, and you would be almost
   next door to me.
Your family too would be comfortable, if there
   were another room in it."
"Yes," he replied, "it is nice to live beside
   friends but, my dear soul, one cannot lodge
   in IF."

---

[1] Book II, v. 739.

XL

SULTĀN MUHAMMAD KHWĀRAZMSHĀH AND THE PEOPLE OF SABZAWĀR[1]

MUHAMMAD Alp Ulugh Khwārazmshāh marched
against Sabzawār, which was a city of refuge
for all rascals.[2]

When his troops had reduced it and were about
to massacre the foe,

They threw themselves at his feet, crying,
"Mercy! Make us thralls, only spare our
lives.

Whatsoever tax and tribute thou mayst demand,
we will pay that and more to thee at every
season.

O lion-hearted King, our lives are thine, but
leave them in trust with us for a little while."

He replied, "Ye shall not save your lives from
me unless ye bring an Abū Bakr into my
presence.[3]

[1] Book V, v. 845. Sultān Muhammad Khwārazmshāh
(1199-1220 A.D.) ruled over a great empire in Central Asia.
He fled before the Mongols and died in exile. Sabzawār
was situated in the Bayhaq district to the west of Nīshāpūr.

[2] Most of its population were fanatical Shī'ites.

[3] Any person bearing the name of the first orthodox
Caliph would be anathema in such a hotbed of heresy.

128

Unless ye bring someone whose name is Abū
Bakr as a gift to me from your city, O mis-
creants,

I will mow you down like corn, ye vile people!
I will accept neither tribute nor fair words."

They offered him many sacks of gold, saying,
"Do not demand an Abū Bakr from a city
like this.

How should there be an Abū Bakr in Sabzawār,
or a dry clod at the bottom of the river?"

The King averted his face from the gold and
said, "O infidels, unless ye present me with
an Abū Bakr,

'Tis of no avail. I am not a child, that I should
stand dumbfounded at the sight of gold and
silver."

O base wretch, until thou prostrate thyself in
prayer thou wilt not be saved, even if thou
shouldst traverse the whole mosque on thy
séant.[1]

They despatched emissaries, right and left, to
search for an Abū Bakr in this God-forsaken
place,

And after three days and nights spent in hurrying to and fro an emaciated man of that name
was discovered.

He was a wayfarer, who had fallen ill: they

[1] This verse is a comment by the poet.

found him lying at the point of death in a
corner of a ruined house.

"Rise up!" they cried; "the Sultān hath summoned thee. Thou wilt be the means of saving
our people from massacre."

He answered, "If my feet could carry me, I
would have gone on to my destination.

How should I have remained in this abode of
my enemies? I would have journeyed towards the city of my friends."

They brought a bier and lifted upon it the Abū
Bakr whom I celebrate,

And the bearers set off to convey him to Khwārazmshāh, in order that the King might behold the sign.

Sabzawār is this world, where the man of God
is abandoned and left to perish.

Khwārazmshāh is God Almighty, who demands
of this unrighteous people the gift of a pure
heart.

XLI

THE MAN WHO WISHED TO LEARN THE LANGUAGE OF BEASTS AND BIRDS[1]

A YOUNG man said to Moses, "Teach me the language of the animals,

That perchance from the voice of animals and wild beasts I may get a lesson concerning my religion.

Since the languages of the children of Adam are entirely for the sake of acquiring wealth and reputation,

It may be that the animals have a different care —namely, to meditate on the hour of passing away from the world."

"Begone," said Moses; "abandon this vain desire, for it is fraught with much danger before and behind.

Seek the religious lesson and the gift of spiritual wakefulness from God, not from books and words and lips."

He answered, "O generous one, 'tis unworthy of thy bounty to disappoint me of the object of my desire.

[1] Book III, *v.* 3266.

131

Thou art the vicegerent of God: if thou prevent me, I shall be in despair."

Moses said, "O Lord, surely the accursed Devil has taken possession of this simple man.

If I teach him, it will be harmful to him; and if I refuse to teach him, he will lose heart."

God said, "Teach him, O Moses, for We in our lovingkindness never reject anyone's prayer.

Grant his wish: let him have a free hand to choose good or evil."

Once more did Moses warn him kindly, saying, "The thing thou desirest will make thy face pale.

Give up this idle passion, fear God! The Devil hath instructed thee for his own cunning purposes."

He replied, "At any rate, teach me the language of the dog at the door and the feathered domestic fowl."

"Hark," said Moses, "thou knowest best! Go, thy wish is granted: the language of both will be revealed to thee."

At daybreak, in order to make trial, he stood waiting on the threshold.

The maid-servant shook the table-cloth; a

piece of bread, the remains of last night's supper, fell out.

A Cock snatched it up, as though it were the stake in a race. The Dog cried, "You have defrauded me.

You can eat corn and barley and other grains, while I cannot, O jubilant one.

And now you deprive the dogs of this little crust of bread, the bread which belongs to us!"

"Hush!" said the Cock, "do not grieve. God will give you something else instead of this.

The Master's horse is about to die: to-morrow eat your fill and be happy.

The horse's death will be a feast-day for the dogs: you will get plenty of food without toil or trouble."

On hearing this speech, the man sold his horse. The Cock was disgraced in the eyes of the Dog.

Next day the Cock carried off the bread as before, and the Dog opened his mouth at him,

Saying, "O deceitful Cock, how long will you tell such lies? You are unrighteous and false and ignoble.

Where is the horse that you said would die? You are like a blind astrologer, your predictions are devoid of truth."

That knowing Cock answered, "His horse died
in another place.

He sold the horse and escaped from loss: he
cast the loss upon others;

But to-morrow his mule will die, and that
will be good luck for the dogs. Say no
more."

The covetous man immediately sold the
mule and delivered himself from grief and
loss.

On the third day the Dog addressed the Cock—
"O prince of liars with your drums and kettle-
drums!"

"Yes," said the Cock, "he sold the mule in
haste; but to-morrow his slave will be stricken
down,

And when his slave dies, the next of kin will
scatter pieces of bread upon the dogs and
beggars."

The Master heard this and sold his slave:
he was saved from loss, he beamed with
joy.

Next day the disappointed Dog said, "O drivel-
ling Cock, where are all those good things
you promised me?

How long, pray, will your falsehood and deceit
continue? Verily, nothing but falsehood flies
out of your nest."

The Cock answered, "Far be it from me and

134

from my kind that we should be afflicted
with falsehood.

We cocks are veracious like the muezzin: we
are observers of the sun and seekers of the
right time.

Though you clap us under an inverted bowl,
we still watch the sun inwardly.

To-morrow the Master himself will certainly die:
his heir will slaughter a cow for the funeral.

High and low will get pieces of bread and
dainties and viands in the midst of the
street."

When the man heard these things, he ran in hot
haste to the door of Moses, with whom God
conversed,

Rubbing his face in the dust from fear, and
crying, " Save me from this doom, O Kalīm!"[1]

Moses said to him, "Go, sell thyself and escape!
Since thou art so clever in avoiding loss, jump
out of the pit of death!

Throw the loss upon true believers! Make thy
purses and scrips double in size!

I beheld in the brick this destiny which to thee
became visible only in the mirror.

The intelligent foresee the end at the beginning,
the foolish see it only at the end."

---

[1] Moses is called Kalīmu'llāh, because God spoke to him
(*kallamahu*) on Mount Sinai.

Once more he made lamentation, saying, "O bounteous one, do not beat me on the head, do not rub into my face the sin I have committed."

Moses replied, "An arrow sped from the Archer's thumbstall, my lad; 'tis not the rule that it should turn back;

But I will crave of God's good dispensation that thou mayst take the Faith with thee at that hour.

When thou hast taken the Faith with thee, thou art living: when thou goest with the Faith thou art enduring for ever."

At the same instant the Master became indisposed: he felt qualms and they brought the basin.

'Tis the qualms of death, not indigestion: how should vomiting avail thee, O foolish ill-fortuned man?

Four persons carried him home: one of his legs was pressed on the other.[1]

At dawn Moses began his orison, crying, "O God, do not take the Faith away from him!

Act in royal fashion, forgive him, though he has sinned and behaved with impudence and transgressed exceedingly."

[1] In the death-agony. Cf. *Qur'ān*, lxxv, 29.

God answered, "Yes, I bestow the Faith upon
him, and if thou wish I will bring him to life
at this moment.
Nay, at this moment I will bring to life all the
dead in the earth for thy sake."

XLII

THE FRIEND WHO SAID "I"[1]

A CERTAIN man knocked at his friend's door:
his friend asked, "Who is there?"

He answered, "I." "Begone," said his friend,
" 'tis too soon: at my table there is no place
for the raw."

How shall the raw one be cooked but in the
fire of absence? What else will deliver him
from hypocrisy?

He turned sorrowfully away, and for a whole
year the flames of separation consumed him;

Then he came back and again paced to and fro
beside the house of his friend.

He knocked at the door with a hundred fears
and reverences, lest any disrespectful word
might escape from his lips.

"Who is there?" cried his friend. He answered,
"Thou, O charmer of all hearts!"

"Now," said the friend, "since thou art I, come
in: there is no room for two I's in this house."

[1] Book I, v. 3056.

XLIII

THE PEOPLE OF SABĀ[1]

I AM reminded of the story of the people of
Sabā—how their balmy zephyr (*sabā*) was
turned into pestilence (*wabā*) by the words
of the foolish.[2]

That kingdom of Sabā resembles the great
big city which you may hear of from children
in their tales.

The children relate tales, but in their tales is
enfolded many a mystery and moral.

Though they tell many ridiculous things, yet
do thou ever seek the treasure that is hidden
in ruins.

Once there was a City very huge and great,[3]
but its size was the size of a saucer, no more
than that.

It was very huge and very broad and very long,
ever so big, as big as an onion.

---

[1] Book III, *v*. 2600. Sabā is the Sheba of the Bible.

[2] The Story of the Sabæans—their frowardness, their ingratitude for the blessings which they enjoyed, and their
consequent destruction—is related in Book III, *v*. 282 foll.

[3] This is "the children's tale." The "City" signifies the
Nature of Man, the microcosm in which the macrocosm is
contained.

The people of ten cities were assembled within
it, but the whole amounted to three fellows
with unwashed faces.

Within it were numberless people and folk, but
the whole of them amounted to three beggarly
fools.

One was very far-sighted and blind—blind
to Solomon and seeing the leg of the
ant;[1]

And the second was very sharp of hearing and exceedingly deaf—a treasure in
which there is not a barley-corn's weight
of gold;

And the third was naked and bare and in-
decent, but the skirts of his raiment were
long.

The blind man said, "Look, an army is approaching: I see what people they are and
how many."

The deaf man said, "Yes; I hear their voices
and know what they are saying openly and
secretly."

The naked man said, "I am afraid they will
cut off something from the length of my
skirt."

The blind man said, "Look, they have come

[1] Referring to the ant which said (*Qur'ān*, xxvii, 18), "*O
ants, go into your dwellings, lest Solomon and his hosts crush
you unawares.*"

near! Arise and let us flee before we suffer blows and chains."

"Yes," said the deaf man, "the noise is getting nearer. Come on, my friends!"

The naked man said, "Alas, they will covet my skirt and cut it off, and I have no protection."

All three left the City and came forth and in their flight entered a Village.[1]

In that Village they found a fat fowl, but not a mite of flesh on it; 'twas pitiful—

A dried-up dead fowl, and its bones had been pecked by crows till they were bare like threads.

They ate thereof as a lion eats of his prey; each of them became surfeited, like an elephant, with eating it.

All three ate thereof and grew mightily fat; they became like three very great and huge elephants,

So that each young man, because of his fatness, was too big to be contained in the world.

Notwithstanding such bigness and seven stout limbs,[2] they sprang forth through a chink in the door and departed.

---

[1] The world.
[2] The seven members of the body: head, breast, belly,. arms and legs.

The way of creaturely death is an invisible way,
it comes not into sight; 'tis a marvellous
place of exit.

Lo, the caravans follow one after another
through this chink which is hidden from view
in the door.

If you look for that chink, you will not find it;
it is extremely unapparent, though there are
so many processions through it.

*Explaining what is signified by the far-sighted
blind man, the deaf man who is sharp of
hearing, and the naked man with the long
skirts.*

Know that Hope is the deaf man who has
often heard of our dying but has never
heard of his own death or regarded his own
decease.

The blind man is Greed: he sees the faults of
others, hair by hair, and tells them from
street to street,

But his blind eyes do not perceive one
mote of his own faults, albeit he is a fault-
finder.

The naked man is afraid that his skirt will be
cut off: how shall anyone cut off the skirt of
a naked man?

He is the Worldling, destitute and terrified: he

possesses nothing, yet he has dread of thieves.

Bare he came and naked he goes, and all the while his heart is bleeding with anguish on account of the thief.

XLIV

IBRĀHĪM SON OF ADHAM[1]

RECLINING on a throne, that renowned King
heard at night a noise of tramping and shrill
cries from the roof.

He heard loud footfalls on the roof of the
palace and said to himself, "Who dares do
this?"

He shouted from the window, "Who goes there?
Methinks, 'tis no man, but a spirit."

A wondrous folk put their heads down from the
roof, saying, "We are going round by night
for the purpose of search."

"Eh, what are ye seeking?" "Camels," said
they. He cried, "Take heed! Whoever sought
a camel on a roof?"

They answered, "Why, then, art thou seeking
God on the throne of empire?"

That was all. None saw him again: he vanished
like a spirit from the sight of man.

[1] Book IV, *v.* 829. Ibrāhīm, son of Adham, of Balkh, a
celebrated ascetic and mystic, lived in the eighth century.
His legend, modelled upon the story of Buddha, makes him
a prince who abandoned his kingdom in order to devote
himself to God.

Although he was in their presence, his real self remained hidden from them: how should people see aught but the beard and dervish-cloak?

XLV

THE MAN WHO PRAYED THAT
HE MIGHT RECEIVE HIS
LIVELIHOOD WITHOUT LABOUR[1]

In the time of the prophet David a certain man,
 before sage and simple alike,
Used always to utter this prayer: "O God,
 bestow on me riches without trouble!
For Thou hast created me a lazybones, a re-
 ceiver of blows, a slow mover, a sluggard,
And one cannot lay upon sore-backed luckless
 donkeys the load carried by horses and mules.
I am lazy and asleep in this world of phenomenal
 being: I sleep in the shade of Thy bounty
 and munificence.
Surely for them that are lazily sleeping in the
 shade Thou hast ordained a livelihood in
 another fashion.
I crave the daily bread that comes without effort
 on my part, for I have no work except prayer."
Thus was he praying for a long while, all day
 until night and all night until morning.
The people laughed at his words, at the folly
 of his hope, and at his importunity:

[1] Book III, *v.* 1450.

146

"Marvellous! What is he saying—this idiot?
Or has somebody given him beng, which produces dementia?

The way to get daily bread is work and toil and
fatigue; God has bestowed on everyone a
handicraft and the power to seek his livelihood.

At present the King and Ruler and Messenger
of God is the prophet David, endowed with
many accomplishments.

Notwithstanding all his glory and majesty,
forasmuch as the favours of the Friend have
chosen him out,

His livelihood does not come to him without
his weaving coats of mail and labouring as a
craftsman.[1]

Now a God-forsaken abandoned wretch like this,
a low scoundrel and outcast from Heaven,

A backslider of this sort desires, without trading,
at once to fill his pockets with gain!"

One would say to him derisively, "Go and get
it! Thy daily bread has arrived, the messenger has brought the good news";

And another would laugh, saying, "Let us
have a share in the gift, O headman of the
village!"

All this abuse and ridicule could not induce
him to desist from his petitioning,

[1] See p. 120, note 2.

147

So that he became celebrated in the town as
  one who looks for cheese in an empty wallet.

One morning, as he was praying with moans
  and sighs, suddenly a cow ran into his house.
She butted with her horns, broke the bolt, and
  jumped into the house; he sprang up and
  bound her legs.
Then he cut her throat without delay, without
  consideration, and without mercy,
And went to the butcher, in order that he might
  rip off her hide forthwith.
The owner of the cow espied him and said,
  "Hey, why did you kill my cow? Fool!
  Brigand! Deal fairly with me."
He said, "God answered my ancient prayer.
  The cow was my portion of daily bread: I
  killed her. That is my reply."
The enraged owner seized him by the collar,
  struck him in the face with his fist several
  times,
And led him to the prophet David, saying,
  "Come, you crazy fool and criminal!
What are you saying? What is this prayer of
  yours? Don't laugh at my head and beard
  and your own too, O rascal!
Hey, gather round, O Muslims! For God's
  sake, how should his prayer make my property
  belong to him?"

The people said, "He speaks truth, and this prayer-monger seeks to act unjustly.

How should such a prayer be the means of acquiring property? Give back the cow or go to prison!"

Meanwhile the poor man was turning his face to Heaven and crying, "None knoweth my spiritual experience save Thee.

Thou didst put the prayer into my heart, Thou didst raise a hundred hopes in my heart.

Not idly was I uttering the prayer: like Joseph, I had dreamed dreams."

When the prophet David came forth, he asked, "What is all this about? What is the matter?"

The plaintiff said, "O prophet of God, give me justice. My cow strayed into his house.

He killed my cow. Ask him why he killed my cow and bid him explain what happened."

David said to the poor man, "Speak! Why did you destroy the property of this honourable person?"

He replied, "O David, for seven years I was engaged, day and night, in supplication and entreaty,

Praying to God that He would give me a lawful means of livelihood without trouble on my part.

After all this calling and crying, suddenly I saw a cow in my house.

My eyes became dim, not on account of the food, but for joy that my supplication had been accepted.

I killed her that I might give alms, in thankfulness that He who knoweth things unseen had hearkened to my prayer."

David said, "Wipe out these words and set forth a legal plea in the dispute.

Who gave you the cow? Did you buy or inherit her? Will you take the crop when you are not the farmer?

You must pay this Muslim his money. Go, try to borrow it, and don't seek to do wrong."

"O King," said the poor man, "thou art telling me the same thing as my oppressors."

Then, prostrating himself, he cried, "O Thou who knowest the ardent faith within me, cast that flame into the heart of David;

Put in his heart that which Thou hast secretly let fall into mine, O Benefactor!"

He said this and began to weep and wail so that David was moved exceedingly.

David said to the plaintiff, "Give me a respite to-day. I will go to a solitary place and commune with God."

He shut the door, and then went quickly to the

prayer-niche and betook himself to the invocation that God answereth.

God revealed all to him, and he saw who was the man deserving of punishment.

Next day, when the litigants assembled and formed ranks before David, the plaintiff lifted up his voice in reproach.

David said to him, "Be silent! Go, abandon your claim, acquit this true believer of responsibility.

Seeing that God has thrown a veil over you, depart in silence and render due thanks unto God for what He has concealed."

He cried, "Oh, woe is me! What wisdom is this, what justice? Wilt thou establish a new law in my case?

Such wrong has never been done even to blind dogs; mountains and rocks are burst asunder by this iniquity."

Then said David, "O contumacious man, give him on the spot all that you possess.

Since 'twas not your fortune to be saved, little by little your wickedness has come to light.

Begone! Your wife and children have now become his slaves. Say no more!"

The plaintiff ran up and down in a frenzy, dashing stones against his breast with both hands,

While the people too began to blame David, for
they were ignorant of the hidden circumstances.

The currish mob, which slays the oppressed
and worships the oppressor, sprang forth
from ambush and rushed towards David,

Crying, "O chosen prophet, this is unworthy
of thee, 'tis manifest injustice; thou hast
abased an innocent man for naught."

He said, "My friends, the time is come for his
hidden secret to be displayed.

Arise, all of you, let us set out, that we may
become acquainted with his mystery.

In such and such a plain there is a huge tree,
its boughs thick and numerous and curved.

Its tent and tent-pegs are very firm; from its
roots the smell of blood is coming to me.

Murder was done at the foot of that goodly
tree: this ill-fated man killed his master.

The crime, which God's mercy concealed till
now, has at last been brought to light through
the ingratitude of this scoundrel,

Who never once looked upon his master's family,
not even at Nawrūz[1] and other seasons of
festival,

And never searched after the destitute children
to relieve their want, or bethought him of the
obligations he had received,

[1] The Persian New Year's Day.

And so proceeded, till for the sake of a cow this
   accursed wretch is now felling his master's
   son to the earth.

He himself has lifted the veil from his crime;
   else God would have kept it hidden.

Wrong is covered up in the depths of the heart:
   the wrong-doer exposes it to men,

Saying, 'Behold me! I have horns! Behold the
   cow of Hell[1] in full view'! "

When they arrived at the tree, David said, "Tie
   his hands fast behind him,

That I may bring his sin to light and plant the
   banner of justice on the field.

O dog," said he, "you killed this man's father.
   You were a slave; by murder you became a
   lord.

You killed your master and seized his property:
   God hath made it manifest.

Your wife was his handmaid: she has acted
   unjustly towards her master.

The children she bore to him, male and female
   —all of them from beginning to end are the
   property of the master's heir.

You are a slave: your goods are his property.
   You have demanded the Law: take the Law
   and go: 'tis well.

[1] The fleshly soul, as is explained in the concluding verses
of the Story.

You killed your master miserably, whilst he
    was crying for mercy on this very spot,
And hastily hid the knife under the soil because
    of the terrible apparition which you beheld.
On the knife, too, the name of this hound is
    written who betrayed and murdered his
    master.
His head together with the knife is beneath!
    Dig ye back the soil, thus!"
Even so they did, and when they cleft the earth
    they found there the knife and the skull.
A tumult of lamentation went up from the
    people: everyone severed the girdle of un-
    belief.[1]
Then David said to him, "Come, O seeker of
    justice, and with that black face of yours re-
    ceive the justice due to you!"
He ordered him to be killed in retaliation with
    the same knife: how should cunning deliver
    him from the knowledge of God?

Kill thy fleshly soul and make the world spiritu-
    ally alive. She hath killed her master: make
    her thy slave.
The slayer of the cow is thy rational spirit: go,
    be not offended with the spirit that kills the
    flesh.

---

[1] Christians, Jews, and Zoroastrians wore a girdle
(*zunnār*) to distinguish them from the Faithful.

154

The spirit is a captive, and craves of God daily bread won without toil, and bounty spread before it on a table.

Upon what does its daily bread depend? Upon its killing the cow, which is the origin of all evil.

XLVI

THE GHUZZ RAIDERS AND THE TWO NOTABLES[1]

THE murderous Ghuzz Turcomans raided a village. They found two notables and were about to put one of them to death.

When they had tied his hands, he said, "O princes and high pillars of the empire,

For what reason do ye seek to slay me? Wherefore, pray, are ye thirsting after my blood?

What is the sense, what is the object, in killing me, when I am so poor and destitute?"

One of the Ghuzz replied, "To strike awe into this friend of yours, so that he may produce his gold."

"Why," said the man, "he is poorer than I." "So he says," replied the Ghuzz, "but he has done it on purpose. He is rich."

"Since it is a matter of opinion," said the man, "he and I are in the same case: the probabilities are equal.

Kill him first, O princes, in order that I may be terrified and point out the way to the gold."

[1] Book II, v. 3046.

XLVII

HĀRŪT AND MĀRŪT[1]

LISTEN to the tale of Hārūt and Mārūt, O thou
to whose face we are devoted slaves.[2]

Hārūt and Mārūt were intoxicated with the
spectacle of God and the marvel of His
gradual temptation of them.

Such intoxication arises from His temptation:
you may judge, then, what intoxications are
wrought by the ascension to God?

If the bait in His snare produces intoxication
like this, what delights will the table of His
bounty reveal!

They were drunken and freed from the noose:
they were uttering rapturous cries in the
fashion of lovers;

But in their road there was an ambush and trial:

---

[1] Book III, *v.* 800. Hārūt and Mārūt were two angels, who
looked with contempt on the sinful state of men and received
permission to visit the earth, though God warned them of the
temptations to which they would be exposed. On coming
down to the earth, they fell in love with a beautiful woman
—Venus, according to some accounts—and seduced her.
Given the choice of punishment in this world or the next,
they preferred the former and were imprisoned in a pit at
Babylon.

[2] Husāmu'ddīn, to whom the *Mathnawī* is dedicated.

157

its mighty wind would sweep away mountains like a straw.

The Divine trial was driving them headlong;
but how should one who is drunken be con-
scious of these things?

To him pit and open field are one, to him dun-
geon and pit are a pleasant path to tread.

The mountain-goat runs up the high mountain
to feed in safety.

While browsing, suddenly he sees another trick
played by the ordinance of Heaven.

He casts his gaze upon another mountain, and
there he espies a she-goat.

Straightway his eyes are darkened: he leaps
madly from this mountain to that.

To him it seems as easy as to run round the
sink in the court of a house.

Those thousands of yards are made to appear to
him as two, in order that from mad infatua-
tion the impulse to leap may come to him.

As soon as he leaps, he falls midway between
the two pitiless mountains.

He had fled to the mountain to escape from the
hunters: his very refuge shed his blood.

Hārūt and Mārūt, being intoxicated with pride,
said, "Ah, we would rain upon the earth, like
clouds;

We would spread in this place of injustice a

carpet of justice and equity and devotion and faithfulness."

So they said; and the Divine Decree was saying to them, "Stop! Before your feet is many an unseen pitfall."

The Decree was saying this, but their ears were muffled in the veil of their hotheadedness.

All eyes and ears are shut, except in them that have escaped from themselves.

Who but Grace shall open the eyes? Who but Love shall allay the Wrath?

XLVIII

THE GRAMMARIAN AND THE BOATMAN[1]

A SELF-CONCEITED grammarian embarked in a
 boat. Turning to the boatman, he asked,
"Have you ever studied grammar?" "No," he
 replied. "Then," said the grammarian, "half
 your life has been lost."
The boatman, heart-broken with grief, refrained
 from answering him at the time.
The wind cast the boat into a whirlpool. The
 boatman shouted to the grammarian,
"Tell me, can you swim?" "No," said he, "O
 fair-spoken, well-favoured man."
"O grammarian," he cried, "your whole life
 is lost, for the boat is sinking in this whirlpool."

Know that here *mahw* (self-naughting) is needed,
 not *nahw* (grammar). If you are *mahw* (dead
 to self), you may plunge into the sea without
 peril.
The sea bears up one who is dead; but if

[1] Book I, *v.* 2835

160

he be living, how shall he escape from the
sea?

When you have died to the fleshly nature, the
sea of divine consciousness will raise you
aloft.

XLIX

THE GARDENER AND THE THREE FRIENDS[1]

A GARDENER found in his orchard three men
who looked like thieves,

A Jurist and a Sharīf[2] and a Sūfī: each one an
impudent, knavish, perfidious rogue.

He said, "I have a hundred arguments against
these fellows, but they are united, and union
is strength.

I cannot cope singly with the three, so first I
will separate them, and when each is alone I
will tear out his moustache."

He employed a ruse to get the Sūfī away and
poison the minds of his friends against him.

"Go to the house," said he, "and fetch a rug
for your comrades."

Then he said to the two friends in private,
"Thou art a Jurist, and thy friend is a renowned Sharīf.

'Tis according to thy legal decision that we eat
our bread, 'tis by the wings of thy knowledge
that we fly;

[1] Book II, v. 2167.
[2] A descendant of the Prophet.

And thy friend is our prince and sovereign: he
is a Sayyid of the Prophet's House.

Who is this gluttonous vile Sūfī that he should
consort with noblemen like you?

When he comes back, beat him off and take
possession of my orchard for a week.

My orchard? Nay, my life. Ye are dear to me
as the apple of my right eye."

He tempted and beguiled them. Ah, one must
not patiently submit to losing one's friend.

When they had driven the Sūfī away, the enemy
went after him with a stout cudgel.

"O dog," he cried, "is it Sūfism that of a sudden
you come into my orchard in spite of me?

Has Junayd[1] or Bāyazīd[2] directed you to behave
so? From what Shaykh did you receive this
instruction?"

Raising his cudgel, he belaboured the helpless
Sūfī, cracked his head and half killed him.

"My score is paid," said the Sūfī, "but have a
care for yourselves, O comrades!

Ye treated me as a foe. Look out! I am not
more unfriendly than this scoundrel.

The cup which I have drunk ye must drink, and
such a draught is what every cad deserves."

Having finished with the Sūfī, the Gardener
devised a pretext of the same kind as before.

[1] Junayd of Baghdād, an eminent Sūfī, died in 911 A.D.
[2] See p. 100, note 1.

"My dear Sharīf," said he, "I have baked some scones for breakfast.

Will you go to the house and bid Qaymāz bring them to us along with the goose?"

Then, turning to the other, "Doctor," said he, " 'tis manifest and sure that thou art skilled in the law;

But thy friend a Sharīf! His claim is absurd. Who knows who committed adultery with his mother?

He has tacked himself on to 'Alī and the Prophet, and in the world there are plenty of fools to believe him."

He spoke plausibly, and the Jurist hearkened to him. Then that insolent bully went after the Sharīf.

"You ass!" he cried, "who invited you into this orchard? Is robbery your inheritance from the Prophet?

The lion's cub resembles the lion: in what respect do you resemble the Prophet? Tell me that!"

The Sharīf was devastated by the blows of that ruffian. He said to the Jurist, "I have got out of the water.

Now you are left alone. Stand fast! Be like a drum and take your beating!

If I am no Sharīf and unworthy of your friendship, at any rate I am no worse for you than such a ruffian as this."

The Gardener came up to the Jurist, saying, "What sort of jurist are you? The veriest fool would be ashamed of you.

Is it your legal opinion, O convicted thief, that you may come into my orchard without asking leave?

Have you read such a licence in the *Wasīt*, or is this question thus decided in the *Muhīt?*"

"You are right," he replied; "give me a drubbing! This is the fit punishment for one who deserts his friends."

L

THE MONK IN SEARCH OF
A MAN [1]

A MONK was seen in the daytime going round
the bazaar with a lighted candle, his heart
filled with love and rapture.

Some busybody said to him, "Hallo, what are
you seeking in every shop?

What is it you are in search of, going round
with a candle in the bright sunshine? What
is the joke?"

He replied, "I am searching everywhere for a
man who is made living by the life of the
spirit.

Is there a man in existence?" "Why," said the
other, "this bazaar is full of men, O noble
sage."

The monk said, "I want one who is a man in
the way of two passions—anger and lust.

Where is he who proves himself a man in the

---

[1] Book V, *v.* 2887. Diogenes Laertius in his *Lives of the
Philosophers* relates this Story of Diogenes the Cynic:
λύχνον μεθ᾽ ἡμέραν ἅψας περιῄει λέγων "ἄνθρωπον
ζητῶ." Phaedrus tells it of Aesop.

hour of anger or lust? In quest of such a man
I am roaming from street to street.
Where in the world shall I find one who is a
man on these two occasions, that I may
sacrifice my life for him to-day?"

LI

THE ECSTASY OF BĀYAZĪD[1]

THAT venerable dervish, Bāyazīd, came to his
disciples and said, "Lo, I am God."

That master of mystic knowledge exclaimed
rapturously, "Hark, there is no god but I, so
worship me."

When the ecstasy had passed, they said to him
at dawn, "Thou saidest such and such, and
it is blasphemous."

He replied, "This time, if I make a scandal,
come on at once and plunge your knives into
me.

God is incorporeal, and I am in the body. Ye
must kill me if I say a thing like that."

Again he became intoxicated by the potent
flagon: these injunctions vanished from his
mind.

The dessert appeared: his reason became distraught. The dawn broke: his candle became useless.

Reason is like the prefect: when the Sultan
arrives, the helpless prefect creeps into a
corner.

[1] Book IV, v. 2102.

Reason is God's shadow: God is the Sun. How can the shadow resist His sun?

When a man is possessed by a spirit, the attributes of humanity disappear from him.

Whatsoever he says is really uttered by the spirit: the speaker on this side is controlled by one belonging to the other side.

A spirit hath such influence and rule: how much more powerful must be the Creator of that spirit!

If a pot-valiant fellow shed the blood of a fierce lion, you will say that the wine did it, not he;

And if he fashion words of pure gold, you will say that the wine has spoken them.

Wine can rouse such transports: hath not the Light of God that virtue and potency

To empty you entirely of self, so that you should be laid low and He should make the Word lofty within you?

Though the *Qur'ān* is from the lips of the Prophet—if anyone says God did not speak it, he is an infidel.

When the *Humā*[1] of selflessness took wing and soared, Bāyazīd began to repeat those ecstatic words.

The flood of bewilderment swept away his

---

[1] The lammergeier or bearded griffon.

reason: he spoke more strongly than he had
spoken at first,

Saying, "Within my mantle there is naught but
God: how long wilt thou seek Him on the
earth or in heaven?"

The disciples, frenzied with horror, dashed
their knives at his holy body.

Like the fanatics of Girdakūh,[1] they were ruth-
lessly stabbing their spiritual Director.

Everyone who plunged a dagger in the Shaykh
made a gash in his own body.

There was no mark of a wound on the body of
the Master, while the disciples were drowned
in blood.

Whoever aimed a blow at his throat saw his
own throat cut and perished miserably;

And whoever struck at his breast, his own
breast was riven, and he became dead for
ever;

And he that was acquainted with that spiritual
emperor of high fortune and had not the
heart to strike a heavy blow,

Half-knowledge tied his hand, so that he saved
his life and only wounded himself.

When day dawned, the disciples were thinned:
wails of lamentation arose from their house.

Thousands of men and women came to Bāyazīd,

---

[1] A stronghold of the terrible sect generally known as the
Assassins.

saying, "O thou in whose single shirt the
two worlds are contained,
If this body of thine were human, it would have
been destroyed, like a human body, by the
daggers."

O you who stab the selfless ones with the sword,
you are stabbing yourself. Beware!
For the selfless one has passed away in God
and is safe: he is dwelling in safety for ever.
His form has passed away, and he has become
a mirror: naught is there but the image of
another face.
If you spit at it, you spit at your own face; and
if you strike at the mirror, you strike at yourself;
And if you see an ugly face in the mirror, 'tis
you; and if you see Jesus and Mary, 'tis you.
He is neither this nor that: he is pure and trans-
parent, he has placed your image before you.

Close thy lips, O my soul: though eloquence is
at thy command, do not breathe a word—
and God best knoweth the right way.